Sunrise Over Abidjan

Josefa Hendrix

*The true story about a Jewish woman saving
one tiny African soul in a war-torn country*

Published by:

Sunrise Press
PO Box 23442
Jerusalem, Israel 97245-01
ashya.hendrix @gmail.com
www.Sunrise-Book.com

Distributed by:

Sunrise Press
PO Box 23442
Jerusalem, Israel 97245-01

Sunrise Press

For: Nesya, who has made my life a joy

For: Yafa Achituv, my mother, who has
given me so much love and showed me
how to be strong

Dedicated in Memory of:

Yosef Achituv, z"l, my father, who
guided me through adulthood

Yehoshua Hefetz, z"l, who knew how
to live life to the fullest

ACKNOWLEDGMENTS:

- LEAH HEFETZ, WHO MADE IT ALL POSSIBLE

- MANI, A WONDERFUL UNCLE, WHO RISKED HIS LIFE

- RACHEL AND DORA, WHO GUIDED ME DURING THE MOST DIFFICULT TIMES

- RACHEL MARTIN, WHO IN HER SPECIAL WAY, GAVE ME DIRECTIONS

- ZE'EV GOLDMAN, ARIEH SUD, SHMUEL SIVAN, ARIENNE LERNER, FOR THEIR SUPPORT

- BENNY AND ETI AMAR, OF DFUS ATID (DFUSATID@SMILE.NET.IL) WHO ENCOURAGED ME AT EVERY STEP OF THE PRODUCTION OF THE BOOK

- DRORA MATLOFSKY AND ZIPPI GRODETSKY FOR THEIR BEAUTIFUL EDITING

- PNINA TADMOR, FOR TRANSLATION OF TADMOR TRANSLATION SERVICES (TADMORTR@NETVISION.NET.IL), WHICH CAPTURED MY THOUGHTS AND FEELINGS IN A VERY VIVID WAY

- A SPECIAL THANKS TO:

  BEIT KNESSET YOSEF HAIM, YOUNG ISRAEL, RAMOT, JERUSALEM

TABLE OF CONTENTS

Sunrise Over Abidjan

Chapter One

First Glance at Mother Africa:
Expectations, Hopes, and Dreams

The pilot announced, "We are now flying over the Sahara Desert." I was amazed at how stark and barren it looked even from a height of 35,000 feet. Yet I knew that within this barrenness thrived a world of life that would never be detected by most people, since only a few brave nomads ever ventured into it. I stretched to see if I could get a glimpse of some living creature, but the desert spread a blanket of invisibility on all its inhabitants. I looked at my watch. In just three and a half hours, I would be landing in Abidjan, the Paris of Africa. I thought about my mission, the culmination of a life-long dream. I tried to imagine the next 24 hours. Would everything go as planned? What would it be like to say, "I did it! I finally did it!"

My attention was drawn to my fellow travelers – so colorful they were, compared to my reserved western dress. The colors were brilliant, the lines chic. Each garment was especially designed for its owner. The accessories were perfectly matched to the garment. The passengers were proud and dignified and seemed happy to be going home. It is said that each individual is a whole world in himself. I surreptitiously strained to see if I could discern the topics of conversation. The appearance of these dignified globe-trotters gave the impression that they had to be discussing issues of great importance. My French, however, was rusty. What I was able to decipher seemed mundane and of no interest to anyone other than those engaging in the conversation.

I must have dozed off, because the next words I heard were the pilot's announcement to prepare for our awaited landing. I fastened my seatbelt and looked out the window to catch my first glimpse of Mother Africa, the primeval nourisher of all life. There she was – as lush and green as she was during Adam's and Eve's visit. I leaned back in my seat, never taking my eyes off of her as we descended from our lofty position in the sky. I felt the pull of gravity, or was it the drawing of a child to its mother's breast. The pulse and rhythm of The Land began to permeate me. It was a familiar feeling, yet a strange feeling. I am not sure why. Maybe, one's DNA always remembers from whence it came. I sat in my seat a few minutes longer as the other passengers collected their personal items from the overhead storage and began to move towards the exit. They continued to blather as they deplaned. Slowly I collected the remains of my carry-on baggage, which had been so rudely snatched from me in the airport in Paris, and walked towards the exit. "Au revoir." "Bonne nuit", the flight attendants said. Carefully, I stepped out onto the descending staircase. My eyes had to adjust to the late afternoon glaring sunlight. The figures at the bottom of the staircase looked like chess pieces scattered upon the tarmac. I tried harder to focus my vision. Who or what were these statues?! Why were they posed in such a threatening way?! Was it disbelief or failing eyesight? Fear gripped my heart. Soldiers, squared-jawed, flaunting sinister stares, were pointing their bayoneted rifles directly at the alighting passengers. I tried hard to collect my thoughts and to discern what was happening. Then I remembered the words of my co-patriot at the Ivory Coast Embassy in Tel-Aviv. Quietly, almost inaudibly, he had informed me, after the clerk processing my visa papers left the room, "You know there are problems there." "What, economic problems?" I asked innocently. "No," he replied." They are under military rule." Not really connecting the Hebrew term to the full English connotation, I had not truly grasped the situation in which I had landed. I tried to organize my thoughts so that I could conduct myself in the most appropriate manner. I tried to stay calm. I wanted to re-unite with my mobile phone and notify people back home of the seriousness of the situation. Why hadn't I remembered to remove my phone from my carry-on before it was so rudely snatched from me at the airport in Paris?

Why were those passengers so eager and happy to go home?! Well, I guess home is home no matter how bad it is.

With sharp feelings of trepidation and strong feelings of doubt and concern, I solidly placed my right foot on the hot asphalt tarmac of Abidjan. I was here for a purpose and I had to continue. Hoping that my sense of fear was not radiating to the camouflage-uniformed soldiers, I weaved in and out between them, making my way towards the terminal. A "Welcome to Abidjan" sign, which hung over the main entrance, shone fire-red as the sunset behind the assortment of corrugated steel structures posing as an airport terminal. A "Sorry, but we are under construction" sign gently swayed in the stifling hot late afternoon breeze. As I entered the building the last rays of the sun disappeared - and so did my hopes for an uneventful trip.

Inside the terminal were four queues for passport control. I could not discern what the division was for the queues; so I stood in the shortest, least congested queue. Soldiers with piercing stone eyes stood at the head of each queue, observing the processing of passports by the puppet-like clerks. No one dared make any unnecessary moves. There was a cluster of soldiers standing by the exit to Baggage Claim. I dreaded the thought of walking between them. I peered at them out of the corner of my eye while pretending to be readying my papers for processing. Everyone in the terminal was under their constant scrutiny and surveillance. Suddenly, I heard a soldier shout out "Viens, come!" as he pointed his finger towards one of the men in line. Turning my head slightly, I saw the fellow step out of the queue and walk towards the group of soldiers. One of them suddenly grabbed him by the collar and shoved him through the passageway. Through the strips of the heavy vinyl partition, I could see him being handcuffed and dragged away. This added a few more amperes to my anxiety level. I stepped forward as the person at the front of my line collected his passport and disappeared in the dark passageway and the people in front of me moved forward to claim the space vacated. All the while, I was peering at the group of soldiers who menacingly guarded the vestibule. I heard that voice again, "Vien, come!" Another man was pulled out of line. I braced myself for the scene I expected to transpire. I was surprised to see that this fellow was greeted with open arms and the traditional kiss, first on the right cheek, then on the left and then on the right cheek again. With a pat on the back, he was allowed to walk through the passageway with dignity. The queues shortened. I hoped I would not be the last to exit. Several more young men were crudely removed from the vestibule. One or two more were escorted through as members of the old-boys club.

There were only seven more people in front of me. I patiently waited my turn, trying to relax a bit and reduce the tension which was pulsating through my veins. The stress on me must have been greater then I had realized, for I thought I heard people speaking Hebrew. I quickly turned around to the four men standing in line behind me. Then I realized I had been mistaken; they were speaking French. Darn it! Something was wrong. I knew I was scared but I also knew I was not crazy. I shifted my weight from one foot to the other and adjusted the bags I was carrying; at the same time I positioned myself in such a way that I could pivot myself more quickly. Just as they began to mumble something in Hebrew, I turned around and said quietly, "Shalom!" All four smiled and said almost in lip-sync, "Shalom." The tallest one asked, "Don't you remember me?" "Yes!" I exclaimed, " from the Ivory Coast Embassy in Tel-Aviv, but you said you were leaving on the eighth, not the fifteenth!" "That's right, but I postponed my trip." Then all four slipped into French. I knew that was a sign that we should end our conversation in order not to attract attention. My body felt less tense as I sighed gently but deeply and moved forward in the queue. It was comforting to know that someone who spoke my language was standing so near me in this frightening place.

Finally, it was my turn to clear passport control. I truly didn't want to relinquish my passport even for this brief moment, for fear I would never see it again. The clerk spoke to me in French, and I answered the best I could, my voice quivering with every syllable. Towards the end of the questioning, the clerk spoke to me in flawless English and wished me an enjoyable stay. I thought to myself, "Yeh, right – with soldiers pointing bayonets at my chest!" I smiled and said, "Merci."

I diverted my eyes and tried to make myself small and invisible as I passed between the soldiers. I gave a quick glance to the left and to the right as I passed through the corridor. I wondered if there was an interrogation room or incarceration hold along the way. It was so dark that I almost had to rely on my sense of touch to get to the adjoining room. The air was permeated with a rank smell of sweat and urine. The room I found myself in was so dimly lit that I had no idea where I was. It was illuminated by naked light bulbs hanging from the rafters. They were probably no more than 40-watt bulbs covered with an accumulation of dust. This gave the multitude of caftan and dashiki clad figures an almost ghost-like appearance as they moved to and fro among the military garb. But ghosts don't make that much noise. The babble in the room was almost deafening. People were shouting at each other in French, English, and local dialects. There were no signs for direction. I wandered around aimlessly, sometimes following in the footsteps of someone who seemed to know where he was going. Then, I would retrace my steps because I still had not found the

Baggage Claims section. At one point I ventured towards an exit. Suddenly, two soldiers placed themselves in front of me, giving me an icy glare. I began to sweat profusely. I said, " eh, Baggage Claim?" I got no response except a finger pointing at the distant mob. I retraced my steps, still unable to locate Baggage Claim. I looked over my shoulder at the two military guards, hoping to get some sign of direction, but they diverted their eyes. A man in civilian clothing emerged from between them. He spoke perfect English. He said to me that it was his official duty to help (for a fee) passengers find their luggage. I asked how much this "service" would cost. He said $20 or 450 C.I. Francs, the local currency. I agreed to pay him $20, since I had no local currency and had no idea how much it was worth. The man said his name was Frank and that he would not leave me until all my belongings were in my possession. He led me to a distant part of the room which was not visible from the passage-way through which I had entered. I looked for a familiar face from the airplane or the Israelis who had stood in queue behind me. Out of the scores of faces only three or four I was sure had been on the same flight. Where had all these other people come from?

Twenty minutes went by and there was no sign of our luggage. Forty minutes passed and still there was no sign. After about an hour and fifteen minutes, a suitcase suddenly plopped on the conveyor belt. All eyes turned towards it. It went all around the belt, disappeared into a dark hole, but no one claimed it. More luggage began to appear and the mad scramble began. The red and green baby stroller-backpack I had brought with me slid down the chute onto the conveyor belt. Frank whisked it off of the belt before in disappeared into the black hole. As people around me began to claim their luggage, I noticed that they were examining it carefully. Soon I realized why. There were signs of tampering. Some pieces of luggage had been so badly rifled through that it could not be closed. The man standing next to me ran his fingers around the lock on his suitcase which obviously had been broken as it was pried open. My two bags arrived. Frank heaved them off of the belt. I checked them for damage or forced entry. Everything seemed to be intact. I was relieved. Suddenly, from behind be I heard a voice call my name. It was Mani, my local contact. He was small in stature but powerful in deeds. He had risked arrest and forced his way into the luggage room. He caught my hand before I placed the $20 bill in Frank's hand. They began to argue. Mani shouted that Frank was pirating help to the unsuspecting and did it right under the noses of the soldiers. Frank pointed to the official looking I.D. card attached to his shirt pocket. Mani retorted that it was fake. Frank was not going to give up so easily. He grabbed my bags. Mani tried to snatch them from him. In all the surrounding cacophony we were beginning to attract attention. A soldier glanced in our direction. I was afraid for Mani. I begged him to let me pay the agreed sum. He looked through the small notes I had in my purse, took out $12 and shoved them in Frank's face. Frank swore at him under his breath and shouted at our backs that he had wasted more than an hour of his working time. Mani turned and gave him a dirty look while he pushed me and my luggage past the sliding glass doors of the exit and on to the steaming pavement which, for me, represented a modicum of safety and freedom.

Later on I learned that $20 was the equivalent of a local's monthly salary.

But now my attention was drawn to more pertinent matters. "Mani, where is she?" I asked. "Over there." He pointed in the direction of a sea of indistinguishable faces – all trying to get a glimpse of their friends or loved ones who had just arrived. Then from among the crowd, a tall regal young African woman stepped forward. Majestically she held in her arms a small bundle. She walked across the street towards us. She looked me directly in the eyes as she placed the precious bundle in my arms. A tear slid down my cheek and landed on the baby's forehead, and then I wept uncontrollably. I had traveled more than 5,000 miles and had waited almost a lifetime for this moment. At this precise moment I had become a mother! With overwhelming gratitude, in soothing Hebrew, I thanked G-d for His goodness, kindness, and mercy.

- -

The long, convoluted ride to Riveria Place – the section of town where we would be spending the night – seemed to stretch on forever. Since the time I had prepared for my departure from Israel, I was "on my feet" for nearly twenty-four hours. I felt a blanket of weariness wrapping itself around me. Every muscle and bone in my body ached. I so much wanted to stretch my tired limbs and lie down on fresh sheets in a bed with fluffy scented pillows. Despite being saturated with fatigue, I did feel an intense surge of satisfaction while enjoying my first minutes of motherhood. Nesya stirred a bit and nestled closer to me, her tiny hand grasping my index finger. I adjusted her in my arms while trying to peer out of the window of the taxi. I strained to concentrate on my surroundings. I wanted a closer look at Mother Africa. All I could see were the distant city streetlights and the silhouette of palm trees along the highway. I tried to keep my mind alert to respond to the issues at hand. My original plan was to go directly from the airport to a hotel, but because of the time it took to extricate myself from the chaos at the airport, it was decided that Nesya and I would sleep at Rachel's flat for the night. Rachel was our local contact person. She was a Liberian who, along with many others, had fled Liberia to the Ivory Coast during the years of turmoil in her home country. Because of her education, she had been able to obtain a fairly good position in an international school where all foreign diplomats sent their children. Her apartment had become the unofficial transit station for Liberians traveling between Liberia and the Ivory Coast. Mani had brought Nesya there from Liberia two days before my arrival. The fact that I was being accompanied by Mani and Dora (Rachel's daughter's au pair) gave me a secure feeling, which alleviated some of my worries about the unexpected change in my agenda. I felt that I was in competent hands. I thought about the moment when I would alight from the plane in Israel and proudly show Nesya to my family and friends.

The taxi swerved as the driver jerked the steering wheel to avoid a pothole in the road. "How much longer is the ride?" I asked Dora, the regal princess who had, by proxy, given me the gift of motherhood. "We have taken a diverting route in order to avoid any chance-meeting with the military rebels. It's longer but much safer." My thoughts were then jerked back to the airport. Yes, this country was under military rule, brought about by a coup d'etat six months prior, when the elected president was forced to flee for his life. I wondered if this event would in any way affect my own personal mission. "Never mind," I thought. "Nesya and I are together, and nothing will ever separate us!"

Finally, after nearly an hour of traveling and retracing our route, we arrived at Riveria Place. Since the taxi driver did not know the exchange rate of the dollar in local currency, we had to look for someone who did. Few stores were open at this hour, especially because of the possibility of attacks by the local militia, the rebels, or the army. We circled around the neighborhood several times, stopping wherever there was a glint of lamp light, asking if we could make a currency exchange. This inconvenience took as long as the ride itself from the airport.

By the time we made the money transaction and stopped in the Riveria Place parking lot my body and brain were numb. Mani held the taxi door open and Dora gently lifted Nesya from my arms. Then, I listlessly alighted from the cab. We tread across a grassy knoll for what would be the first time of many such experiences. The darkness of the night was almost thick enough to grasp hold of. The only lights which could be seen were those in a few of the apartments in the surrounding courtyard. Later, I discovered that this was as much a security measure as it was the result of the looting and rioting which had occurred in the area three months earlier. Once we reached the entrance to Rachel's building, we had to literally feel our way along the stairwell as we climbed the five flights of stairs. After the first flight of stairs, I decided to try to improve my ability to navigate in the darkness; so, I counted the number of stairs in each section. This way I would not be surprised by too many or too few steps and fall flat on my face. The building was eleven stories high, and its elevator had not been operable for as long as most of the residents could remember.

When we arrived at Rachel's apartment, it was nearly one o'clock in the morning. For some reason, I felt rejuvenated. There was so much for me to absorb in my new surroundings – the people, the culture. I am sure that when I arrived in Israel some twenty years ago, I had the same wide-eyed, bewildered look on my face. Rachel greeted us with the traditional African welcome. Though this greeting was similar to the traditional Oriental Jewish salutation to which I was accustomed, I was awkward in my attempt to reciprocate it. While Dora and Mani took Nesya to prepare her for bed, Rachel introduced me to the assortment of guests she was hosting. I had no idea how many rooms were in Rachel's flat, but there were at least 11 people whom she was hosting and several more who had dropped by for the evening parlance. Rachel introduced me to each guest. With a nod of the head and a soft "hello," each one greeted me. I had always been impressed by African regality and self-pride that I had seen in students studying in universities in the U.S.A., and here it was being acted out in its native habitat. There was something intrinsically different between African demeanor and African-American demeanor. One of the young men offered me his seat. Everyone present continued to smile at me after I was seated. I was not sure what was the social etiquette and how to respond; so, I just smiled back at them. Then, someone touched the remote control of the television, and everyone became interested in a soccer game. Rachel sat down near me and asked if there was anything I needed. "Nothing at all," I replied, " but I am truly grateful for your help and your kindness." Rachel bowed her head in response. Dora came from the kitchen with cold drinks for everyone. Again, I was impressed by her regal composure. As I drank my first drink in Africa, I realized that it had been several hours since I had had anything to eat or drink – actually since I was on the plane eleven hours earlier. The drink was soothing, but it was like a drop on the dry desert ground. Dora seemed to sense my needs, and she refilled my glass. I sighed deeply as I finished drinking the contents of the glass. Accompanying the drinks were plates of roasted nuts. Trying not to be too obvious, I observed the scene around me. Besides the sofa, there were two armchairs situated to the left of it, just under large windows from which a lagoon could usually be seen in the distance – and also the *sunrise over Abidjan.* To the right of the sofa, there was one simple dining room chair, and next to it stood a floor lamp and a very worn bookcase on which there was a boom-box and several tapes. The shelves were sparsely filled with books in French and in English. One large book was leaning on the rest. It was the Bible. Near the wall facing the sofa was an octagonal dining room table covered with a white lace table cloth. A large vase with beautiful tropical lilies stood in the middle. Next to the dining room table was a hallway leading to another part of the flat. The outer wall of the hallway was the wall adjacent to the veranda. Besides being a place to sit during the afternoon hours, its main usage was to hang laundry to dry. Later on, I would understand the magnitude of its usage.

Some of the eleven guests were seated on the sofa and chairs, while others were sprawled around on what was once a lush wall-to-wall carpet. Every now and then, someone would make a comment about the soccer game. It was difficult for me to follow what the sports commentator was saying, but I could visually follow what was happening. Actually, because the chair I was sitting on had a wobbly straight back, it was nearly impossible for me to relax and concentrate on the game. Despite this discomfort, I began to doze. A hand, which had been gently place on my shoulder, woke me up. I saw Rachel smiling at me. She said she had prepared a bed for me. Before she could take me to my sleeping quarters, we heard Nesya crying in the adjacent room. Mani jumped up from his place on the floor near the sofa. He ran to bring her to me. Nesya stretched her tiny arms to me. I took her, held her up high and then cradled her in my arms. Rachel told Dora to bring a camera. Nesya and I had our first picture taken together. A warm feeling of joy flowed through me. I had never experienced joy of this kind and of this intensity. It filled the nucleus of every cell in my body. I wondered what little Nesya was experiencing. Dora had prepared formula for her in a baby bottle. I gave Nesya the bottle as Rachel led me to the room where we would be sleeping for the night. It was Rachel's decision that we should sleep in her bed. I tried to protest, but she insisted. She placed Nesya between a stack of pillows on the bed. The bed itself was enormous and quite appropriate for the size of the room. Adjoining the bedroom was a bathroom. It was obvious that this was the master bedroom. Rachel had tried to make it as pleasant and comfortable as she could. Fresh towels and flower-shaped soap had been placed on the bedspread which had been turned back as is the custom in hotels. I tried again to decline the imposition, but she was unrelenting. Rachel smiled, said, "Good night," and closed the bedroom door. I looked at the bed. It was so enticing. Pillows with ruffled, flower-covered pillow cases beckoned me to lay my weary head upon them. I had wanted to shower before going to bed, but this was impossible. Being a slightly spoiled **JA'AP** (i.e. Jewish African-American Princess), I could not shower in cold water. There was no hot water because the heating system was not working. In order to bath, water had to be heated in pots on the kitchen stove, carried to the bathroom, and poured into a large round blue plastic tub. Beside the plastic tub was a handmade wooden stool to sit on. A water pitcher was used to pour water over the body. I certainly was not up to this long procedure, at least not at three o'clock in the morning. It was probably just as well, because once I had donned my night-gown and crawled in between the sheets, I discovered why many Africans prefer to shower in the morning. The whole bed was damp form humidity. The pillows and sheets smelled of mold and mildew. I tossed and turned, trying to find a part of the bed where the smell was less strong. I shuffled the pillows, trying to find one which did not have this stifling smell. My nostrils were choked from the odor. Only because of sheer exhaustion was I able to fall asleep. Nesya was already sleeping soundly, but before I dozed off, I whispered the night prayer in her little ear.

Chapter Two

Introduction to Motherhood

Morning came sooner than I wanted it to, after having been up twice during the night. Still I felt it was important to get into some kind of routine in my new role as a mother. For the first feedings, Dora and Rachel guided and assisted me in measuring the formula and preparing bottles. Mani, still not ready to relinquish his role as surrogate father, fed her as I prepared her bath water. I think he might have regretted it when she threw-up everything she had eaten all over him and herself. Together, we removed her soiled clothing, and I took her to bathe her. Alarm paralyzed my maternal satisfaction. The palms of her tiny hands were bright orange! I quickly checked the soles of her feet. They were also bright orange! I scooped her into my arms and ran to show Mani, Dora, and Rachel this abnormality. Dora calmly stated, "Your baby has malaria. We must immediately take her to the hospital." My heart sank into an abyss of fear from the knowledge that my daughter was seriously ill. I was a mother for less than twenty-four hours, and already I was faced with a crisis situation. I tried to collect my wits and pull my thoughts together in order to deal with this terrifying ordeal. I fumbled around trying to find something to wear, while I mentally went through the impending scenario I would have to face. I had never been in Africa before; so I didn't have the slightest idea what the local medical care would be like. Would it be adequate? Would I be able to afford it? I did not have medical coverage for her because, not knowing her passport number, I was unable to pre-arrange insurance. Would she be hospitalized, and if so, for how long? Stress was overcoming my ability to function. I commanded myself sternly to snap out of it and to pull myself together. Certainly, there would be other crises in motherhood. I must prove to myself and, maybe, to others that I was capable of handling one of those demands.

Finally, we were all prepared for the trip to the hospital. Rachel said she felt that Dora could interpret for me, fill-out forms and handle whatever was necessary. She, herself, had to attend to some other pressing issues. Mani, despite his compact size, was as strong in character as a mighty rock. He had been in the country for only 48 hours, and yet, he knew his way around. He ran down the five flights of stairs and out to the street to flag down a taxi. Dora carried Nesya down the stairs of the dark hallway. I was still astonished by the fact that this had once been a luxurious building. After years of neglect (once the foreign residents had moved out) only the façade of the building testified to its past grandeur. I groped my way along the wall, gingerly using my other senses rather than my sight to descend the five flights of stairs and exit the building. I paused for a moment so that my eyes could adjust to the bright summer morning sunlight. Once outside the building, Dora handed Nesya to me and ran ahead to negotiate the fare with the taxi driver. I hurried as best I could across the sand dunes to the waiting taxi. Mani held Nesya as I crouched to get in the orange-red taxi of indistinguishable origin. It looked like a car that a child would draw. It had a square frame and four treadless tires. Once inside, I noticed that the driver was barefoot. We squeaked and rattled down the palm-lined, dust covered streets. This was my first daylight view of Africa, in general, and of Abidjan in particular. I tried to absorb the sights around me, but I was too distraught to take-in what I saw. We sped down a main boulevard and made a left turn onto a secondary road. Immediately, we left behind the mendicancy of Cocodey Boulevard and drove along a well-pruned wealthy suburban street. I looked out the back window to get a quick glimpse of a beggar on Cocodey Boulevard. Then, I turned my head to look forward at the contrasting landscape sprawled out in front of us. Within a distance of a few meters, we went from a poverty stricken neighborhood to a suburb of huge walled villas. Was this some kind of African enchantment? Dora was giving the taxi driver final instructions for getting to the hospital. He turned right, into a small parking lot surrounded by the foreboding walls of private homes. At the far end of the parking lot was a large building that looked more like a private house than a hospital. I gave Dora money to pay the driver. Mani helped me with Nesya. I stood for a moment to gather my strength for what lie ahead and also to pull myself out of this awful nightmarish situation. We walked through a small but magnificent, lush hedged garden with tropical birds fluttering and chirping. I could have enjoyed this tiny piece of paradise if it were not for the situation. We stepped through sliding glass doors into a freshly scrubbed air-conditioned waiting room, filled with toys of all sizes and assortment. All those waiting greeted us with "Bonjour." I glanced around at the mixture of people. Some were very well-dressed, in European clothes. Others wore tattered clothes. But all were immaculately clean. The children mingled and played as they waited their turn.

Dora entered the nurses' reception station and explained what the urgency was. Then the nurse turned to me and asked me a few questions and gave me forms to fill-out. I was thankful for the high school French I had learned. I was able to fill-out the forms and answer basic questions without too much effort. We were asked to pay a fee and wait outside in the reception room. Nurses and doctors walked back and forth to the inner rooms. As they passed through the waiting room, they stopped and talked with the children and parents. Sometimes they placed a hand on a shoulder to calm fears. A small boy with big brown eyes, who seemed to be on the verge of tears, slowly allowed a smile to spread across his face as he looked into the gentle eyes of an Asian doctor. A European doctor bent down and commended a five-year old girl of mixed descent on her building-block construction. An African doctor bantered with a group of children who were trying to determine "just what was the purpose of that strange object hanging from the ceiling." It seemed to be some sort of mobile, whose sole purpose was to keep the young patients entertained or distracted. Every racial group was represented in this clinic/hospital. Every social strata was represented in this 50-meter area. There were Africans, Europeans, and Asians, both as patients and as staff. Pride and dignity permeated the atmosphere of this medical center. I had always envisioned Africa to be this way, and this element of self-pride helped assuage any feelings of uncertainty I had.

After a brief wait, we were called into the examination

room where Nesya was weighed and measured, and her temperature was taken, rectally. I looked at the baby scale on which she was placed. The needle swung back and forth before settling on 8 and half pounds. I stared in shock. She was a year and a half old and weighed so little. I checked her birth certificate. In the space for weight 12 pounds had been hand-written! I was totally confused.

We were asked to sit and wait, while Nesya's papers were transferred upstairs. I looked around at the healthy babies and toddlers who were there for routine check-ups. Almost unconsciously I began to run my hands along Nesya's small torso. There was hardly a spot that was not covered with festering mosquito bites. There must have been hundreds along her legs and arms. She had barely stopped crying from the rude intrusion of the rectal thermometer, when we were told to go up to the second floor, where doctors would examine her. I tried to soothe her and comfort her, but my inexperienced hands just made her more fretful. Dora gently lifted her and placed her on her shoulder. Nesya immediately quieted down. Was it the strange winding staircase or was it the stress that made me dizzy?

If the first floor was a fine mesh of African-European culture, the second floor had an American motif. The walls were decorated with three-dimensional Walt Disney characters –large, lively and colorful. While we waited, Mani entertained Nesya by carrying her from one figure to the other and allowed her to squeeze noses and pull ears. Mani, who had never been to the U.S., knew the names of all the characters, even all Seven Dwarfs. I admired the way he handled Nesya – very maternal, indeed.

After what seemed like hours, we were finally called into the doctor's office. I could not tell if their stern demeanor was due to professionalism or coldness. They were very businesslike, without any appealing warm "bedside" manner. The atmosphere was so different than the friendly one I had observed on the first floor. This puzzled me. The female European doctor fired questions at Dora. At first she answered them with her usual composure. Then I could see that she was becoming agitated. She fired back answers, her voice rising in timbre. I only understood about 70% of what was being said, but I knew that the questioning was accusative. I interrupted the verbal melee and said in the best French I possessed, "Excuse me, but we came here to get medical treatment for my daughter." The doctor raised her eyebrow as if questioning the audacity of my statement. With a definite condescending tone, she retorted, "This child is very sick. She has a very bad case of malaria and is on the verge of death. She might live and she might not. The next 24- 48 hours are critical. If she makes it through that, she will probably live. We will do blood tests now, but we will not wait for the results; we will start treatment immediately. Take this slip downstairs to the nurses station." My head was swooning. I heard myself say, "Oh! My first 24 hours as a mother!" "Quoi?!" exclaimed the doctor. "I just adopted her, and she came into my care less than 24 hours ago." The doctor, who had been so indignant to us, looked shocked. She and the African doctor, who was leaning against the examining table and observing this whole scene, looked at each other in disbelief. "Could you repeat that?" he asked with a controlled British accent. "This is my first 24 hours as a mother. Nesya is my newly adopted daughter." The two doctors stared at each other. Dr. Quanton, relaxed her posture. Her shoulders dropped into a softer position, and with it, her voice also softened. "We hope your daughter will be fine." I was so totally drained I didn't even say, "Thank you."

We descended the spiral staircase. I fought to keep my balance. At the nurses' station we paid for the Comaquin injections and went to the treatment room for them to be administered. The nurse showed me how to hold Nesya, while she injected the life-saving serum into Nesya's tiny left buttock. She gasped a piercing, heart-wrenching cry and tried to free herself from the source of the pain. I closed my eyes (not wanting to cry) and held her tightly. "My first 24 hours as a mother! Is this the way we must bond – through pain and suffering?"

As soon as we arrived back at Rachel's, one of the house guests informed us that the hospital had called. Though she was completely fluent in French, she said she had trouble understanding the doctor because she seemed so flustered. She said that all she could make out was the word "grosse" which the doctor kept repeating. Dora immediately called the doctor. I just sat on the worn living room sofa, holding Nesya, and staring at her weak body. When Dora hung up the phone her face looked ashened. The worry on her face completely altered her beautiful features. "The doctor," she began," . . . says that Nesya has enough malaria in her system to kill a full-grown adult male." My body and my senses were completely numb. I felt as if I was observing some kind of play written by Charles Dickens. Had I traveled 3,000 miles for my trip to end with a tragedy? Would I be burying my tiny daughter, instead of taking her home to the City of the Patriarchs, to Kiryat-Arba/Hevron?

The next 24 hours were almost more than I could bear. I lay on the bed, wrapped around Nesya in a fetal position. She slept 14 hours, hardly moving a muscle. She sweated profusely, and so did I. I woke her every three hours to give her her oral medication. Immediately afterwards, she would fall back to sleep. I wondered, worried, wept, and prayed that G-d would spare her life.

And so He did. After 14 hours she began to stir on her own. Groggily she opened her eyes and stared into mine. I drew her close to me and hugged her tightly. Her tiny right hand reached for my cheek. I kissed it gently. She ran it across my dry, parched lips. For some reason, at that point, I knew she was going to live. I called for Dora, Rachel, and Mani to come and have a look. They stood silently, looking at the two of us. A slight smile appeared on Rachel's face. Dora rested her hand on Nesya's forehead. Mani said what everyone was thinking, "Well, I guess the worst is behind us. G-d has spared her life. She is going to live." Quietly, I responded, "Toda la-El. (Thank G-d!) "

The next ten days were very hectic. Twice daily we had to drive to the Cocodey clinic for Nesya's injection. By the third injection, she did not even cry, but it was still difficult to see her subjected to such pain so often. Mani and Dora took turns holding her for the injection. Afterwards, they would hand her to me and I would gently rock her and sing her a lullaby.

It was difficult enough trying to cope with our predicament, and the news broadcasts were becoming even more disturbing. They centered around the political situation and the military leader who had appointed himself president after the last coup d'etat. He was aware that he had a strong opposition; so he appeared on television frequently to reassure the public that there would be elections soon. It was of utmost importance that I confirm my return flight. Every time I called the Air France office, I got conflicting information. Finally, I asked Dora if she would accompany me to the airline's office to personally confirm my flight. The sight that we saw was more disturbing than the news broadcasts. Hundreds for foreign nationals were trying to press their way into the airline office to assure their booked flight. Dora said in a serious voice that anyone who had a foreign passport was trying to flee before the election because it was certain that there would be a "coup" afterwards. The prospect of this peril made me shiver inside. When we were finally able to get to the reservation desk, Dora did all the talking. Ever since the doctor had said the word "*tuer*" (in French "to kill") I had lost all ability to understand French, much less speak it. My return flight was booked for the date I had originally scheduled. I was relieved to have that settled. A new sense of hope had returned to me. I was a bit concerned about taking Nesya to Israel in her current medical condition, but I was more concerned about staying in Abidjan, knowing that war could break out any day now.

After leaving the Air France office, we returned to the medical center for Nesya's afternoon injection. Dora interpreted for me when we went to the medical center.

The doctors gave us a medical release statement so we could travel, and prescriptions and instructions for the doctors in Israel. My journey was about to come to an end! . . . . so I thought.

On the way back to Riveria Place, we stopped at the open-air market so that I could buy a few souvenirs. I found a really cute two-piece red outfit for Nesya, probably the last native garment she would have. My heart began to fill with excitement. Soon we would be going home. Some day I would tell Nesya about her ordeal in Africa. Maybe I would even bring her back for a visit. But now, all I wanted to do was to plant us firmly on holy ground.

When we arrived at Rachel's place, I began to organize my belongings for the **_flight home!_** Most of the kosher food which I had brought had been eaten, but I still had plenty of matza. Rachel had shown interest in the unleavened bread from the Holy Land. She was a devout Christian, and I knew it would mean a lot to her to receive it as a gift; so, I gave it to her, along with the money I would have paid to stay in a hotel. Touched by my gesture, she clutched the package to her chest. For Mani and Dora, I felt it was most appropriate to also give them money.

That evening, we sat in the living room, listening to music, while the sun set over Abidjan. Nesya especially liked me to stand near the big picture window as the last rays of the setting sun made the lagoon look like a huge gold coin. Nesya would rest her soft cheek on mine, and I would sing her a lullaby. After the sun set, all of us (including the house guests) sat around the television, watching the evening soccer games and the news reports. Most of the news was in French and of local interest. Very little news was about world affairs. I felt cut-off from what was happening in Israel. I took comfort in the fact that I soon would be back in Israel. Re-adjusting myself on the sofa, I tried to enjoy my last few hours in Abidjan, in the Ivory Coast, and in the bosom of Mother Africa.

Looking at my watch, I saw that in two hours the taxi would arrive to take us to the airport. In a corner of my heart, there was a twinge of sadness. Yes, I was eager to go home, but I also realized that I would be parting from people who had, in a very short time, become such an important part of my life. Breathing deeply, I tried to fill my lungs, and thus, my arteries, with a bit of the specialness that permeated the atmosphere in Rachel's home. I wanted to somehow take a small portion of this specialness home with me.

One of the guests began to hum a tune. Another guest joined her. One by one, everyone present began to hum the melody in perfect harmony. Shortly, the whole room was filled with a cappella singing, in a mixture of English and a native dialect.

The taxi arrived, and Dora and Mani helped me gather up my possessions. Rachel hugged me, and the others wished me well. I picked up Nesya from her make-shift bed and carried her down the five flights of stairs, which by now I was an expert at doing. Once inside the taxi, I looked out the window and tried to photograph in my mind the scenery I would probably never see again.

Nightmares come and nightmares go. The one persistent factor is the unpredictability of their occurrence. The chaos at the airport did not forewarn me. Even the increased presence of soldiers did not clue me in to what was about to happen. The queues stretched into the parking lots opposite the terminal. We had arrived more than two hours before boarding, which should have been enough time. Once near the terminal the soldiers were separating passengers according to their own military criteria. Even Dora could not figure out what was happening. Mani forced his way into the terminal carrying Nesya in his arms. The soldiers pushed him outside, saying "No ticket, no entry." At this point I was on my own, trying to ascertain what was happening and at the same time decipher what was being shouted at me in French. Finally, I stood in front of passport control. The clerk looked at my American passport and stamped it for "Entry", so that I could enter the De Gaulle Airport in Paris. Then I handed him Nesya's passport. He scrutinized it carefully, wrapped our tickets around it and handed them back to me. "She can't fly," he said. Instead of responding in French, I replied in Hebrew, "Ma?" Again he said,

"She can't fly. You can if you want, but she can't fly with you." "Pourquoi?" I managed to blurt out in French.

"She doesn't have a visa."

"Un visa?"

"You must have a visa for her in order to enter France."

"But we are not <u>entering</u> France. We are only passing through."

"Yes. That is called a transit visa."

"She is only a year and a half, and there is only four hours between our   two flights."

"It doesn't matter. She needs a transit visa."

"Before I left Israel, my travel agent checked, and the rules were if the stay was less than 48 hours, no visa is needed."

"Well, our rules are different. Please, step out of line. Here is a form for you to reschedule your flight. Tomorrow go to the French Embassy and request a transit visa . . . "

I could not comprehend what was happening to us. I stood there totally stupefied. What was I to do? Where was I to go? Were Dora and Mani still in the vicinity? How would I find them or contact them? I cursed the person who had stolen my mobile phone from my luggage. At least if I had had my phone, I could contact Dora or Mani or Rachel immediately. Alarm flooded my brain, and I could hardly think. ***What was I going to do?!***

Nesya flopped unsteadily in the baby carriage-backpack. She had fallen asleep on my shoulder. I struggled with my luggage, her diaper bag and her on my back. I was bewildered and frightened. Terrifying thoughts shot through my brain. "How was I going to maneuver? How was I going to be able to inform Mani and Dora of what had happened? Why hadn't I had enough forethought to remove my international cellular phone from my carry-on luggage before it was so rudely ripped out of my hands just before I boarded my Air France flight in Paris? That phone could have saved me from this horrible plight."

Somehow, I found myself standing outside the air terminal. I stood for a moment, staring into the crowd of people who were forced to wait across the street – " for security measures." Then I heard a voice call my name. It was Mani! He broke through the police barrier and ran towards me. He took Nesya from the backpack, cradled her in one arm and pulled my luggage with the other.

"What happened?!" he exclaimed. I couldn't talk. I fumbled for words. Then I handed him the refusal form stating the reason being lack of a transit visa. Dora broke out from the police barrier as we approached. Mani showed her the paper.

"Ridiculous! Are they crazy!"

The refusal slip had to be taken to an Air France hut adjacent to the terminal. The hut was already filled with people trying to re-schedule their flight. People roamed to and fro, trying to find the appropriate queue, clerk, or Air France representative to assist them. The level of tension was high enough to shatter glass. My lack of ability to communicate in French hampered my efforts to seek assistance. Because of the multitude of would-be travelers, soldiers would allow only those with cancelled tickets to enter the premises. I pushed my way out of the crowd to look for Mani and Dora. The desperate look on my face told them that they had to intervene. Dora spoke to the guards and explained my problem. The guards allowed both Mani and Dora to enter with me and Nesya.

After what seemed like an eternity, we finally were able to speak with someone who would even look at my refusal slip. After scrutinizing it carefully, we were told that I could re-schedule my flight only after I had obtained Nesya's visa. This was in direct conflict with what the Air France representative had said in the terminal. I had been told to go immediately to this hut to re-book my flight and, with my new ticket to go to the French Embassy. Hours had passed since we arrived at the airport, and it was nearly midnight. Hope- turned- to- despair penetrated the sultry darkness. Again, the four of us found ourselves sitting in a taxi, heading towards Riveria Place.

We rode back in silence to Riveria Place. In silence, we climbed the dark staircase to Rachel's apartment. Dora opened the door, and Rachel stared at us - in silence.

Chapter Three

The French Embassy

Despite last night's disappointment, I was naively optimistic about getting an expedited visa to go along with my new flight reservation. After taking Nesya to the Cocodey clinic for her morning injection, we headed straight for the French Embassy in downtown Abidjan. Two and a half blocks before the embassy, we noticed people lined up on both sides of the street. Only when the taxi stopped opposite the main gate to the embassy did we realize that *all* of those people were trying to get into the embassy to get visas. We stood and looked in astonishment at the throng of people. It was 8:15 a.m. I wondered when they had arrived. I estimated that there must have been 500 people waiting outside the embassy compound. We tried to figure out where the line began and where it ended. Finally, we placed ourselves close to the electronic gate where a guard stood. Mani approached him to ask about getting a visa. The guard was ill-tempered, rude and not willing to give any information. Since Dora spoke French, she tried her luck. He still was not very helpful. All she could pry out of him was that we had to be on a list. When she asked him what list and how to get on the list, he shouted at her and shoved her away. Since I was carrying Nesya and had a copy of my flight reservation, I decided to try my luck. He barked at me in French, but Dora was able to decipher what he said. He had said to go across the street to one of the "telephone operators" sitting outside the kiosk and call the embassy to ask to be put on the list. There were four such stations. The clerks sat on low wicker foot stools behind desks that looked like they had been confiscated from a local kindergarten. In front of each station there were at least 11 people waiting to be served. We soon discovered that in order to use their services, we had to have written on a piece of paper the number which we wanted them to dial. Once the number was handed to them, they looked through a computer printout (which they kept far away from the public's view), and then, they said how much money it would cost to dial it. Once the money was paid, names and the desired numbers were written on a log-in sheet. We did not have the French Embassy's number. Since we had been referred to them, we thought they would have the number. With little interest in our plight, they just pointed to the guard who had been so rude to us.

We fought our way through the crowd and tried to regain the position we had had. It was now 9:30 a.m., and we were in no better position than we had been when we arrived. The mob began to move forward as if they were about to storm the embassy. The guard roared at everyone and called someone on his walkie-talkie. More guards came out of the embassy as reinforcement. They posed themselves at strategic positions. The glare in their eyes was fierce but unfocused. Standing with legs straddled and arms folded, they took on a daunting stature. En masse, the mob moved back.

At just about the same time, an official looking car pulled-up in front of the gate. The head guard roared for the crowd to move back so that the car could enter. The driver handed the guard some document and then drove into the embassy compound. More cars arrived at the gate; some were limousines and some were ordinary cars. The type of car didn't seem to matter. What was important was that they had the right papers, which allowed their entry.

It was now 10:30, and none of the people who were standing outside in the hot sun had been admitted. At around 11:00, a guard came out of the embassy building, walked over to the head guard and handed him approximately ten pages of computer print-outs. After perusing the pages, the guard began to call out names. No one answered to the first name, nor to the second or the third name. People in the crowd began asking each other what the guard was doing. Finally, after about 15 names, a person jumped forward, shouting. "C'est moi!" (i.e. "It's me'") This person handed the guard some document, and after examining the computer print-out again, the guard allowed the person to stand near the electronic pedestrian gate. A few minutes later, the gate opened, and he was allowed to enter the embassy premises. The guard continued the roll-call. After about 50 more names, five people jumped forward as a group, waving documents in the air. The broad smiles on their faces said more than any words could say. They, too, were allowed to enter the compound. This procedure repeated itself until 12 o'clock. At that time, the guard folded-up the list and turned to enter the embassy compound. The mob charged towards him. He looked at them with disdain and shrieked that the embassy was closed for the day. People began shouting at him in every language imaginable. He was not fazed by this. As he turned around and walked away, he spewed out, "Come back tomorrow!" The crowd stood in silence like stone statues. No one seemed to understand what they had just witnessed. No one knew how to re-act. Hesitantly, these "statues" returned to life, and the people began to disperse into the streets surrounding the embassy.

Still trying to re-gain my senses, the magnitude of this nightmare fell heavily on my shoulders. I feared that I could be stuck in this chaotic bureaucratic maze for days. I was petrified of the ramifications. Thoughts raced through my brain like freed atoms. I needed to formulate a plan to free myself from this Kafka scenario, but no answers burst forth from my distraught mind. I had had enough stress for one day, and I was sure that those with me felt the same.

We stopped the first available taxi and got in. Once inside, we slouched down in the hot, sweaty seats and simply stared at the skyline. It was easy to understand why Abidjan was called, "The Paris of Africa." The landscape was beautiful. The buildings were tall, spacious, and well-designed. With grandeur, they printed their images in the skyline. The city's boulevards were full of exotic tropical flowers and tall palm trees. The beauty of these boulevards was so exquisite that they competed with the beauty of the buildings surrounding them. One building, however, did stand out because of its especially unique architecture. It was built in the shape of a pyramid, and its thatched, A-lined roof was most impressive. Being located at the end of a highway, leading up to the town center, it immediately caught the traveler's attention. This building also overlooked the lagoon, around which Abidjan had grown. At the far-end of the lagoon were luxurious beach houses, restaurants, and yachts at the docks – very much reminiscent of the French Riviera. However, despite the city's past splendor, wear-and-tear had taken its toll on the city's charm. This tarnished luster reminded me of a person, once rich and famous, who had lost his wealth, and the only thing that remained from his heydays was a 30-year-old, well-worn coat, which he was still trying to wear with dignity.

Though thoroughly exhausted from our day's ordeal, we still had to make a detour on the way back to Riveria Place. Nesya was still getting treatment for Malaria and for malnutrition. Our daily routine started by going to the Cocodey clinic for the morning injection, and it ended by returning to the clinic for the afternoon injection. At least it was comforting to know that the level of parasites in her blood had greatly declined. She was well on the way to recovery. There was hardly a place on her body, which <u>was not covered</u> with puss-filled mosquito bites, but they were beginning to heal. Her tummy was still bloated from malnutrition, but it was now soft to the touch and not hard as a rock. The sad look was slowly disappearing from her eyes, and every now and then she did smile. The doctors had told me that soon her eye lashes and eye brows would begin to grow in. Despite her frailty, Nesya was able to walk on her skinny little legs. Mani had bought Nesya her first pair of shoes – little brown sandals. Rachel, however, was a little disturbed by his choice, because she felt that Nesya needed sandals that gave more support to her tiny legs; so, Rachel bought her another pair of sandals – red high tops, which were much easier to keep on her feet. To everyone's satisfaction, Nesya was beginning to eat solid food and was gaining some weight.

Once back at Riveria Place, Rachel, Dora, Mani, and I sat down to work out a strategy to get into the French Embassy to get Nesy'a visa. This was our proposed agenda:

a) Call Air France to reserve a flight.

b) Locate the French Embassy phone number.

c) Find out how to get on the list to enter the embassy.

d) Try to make arrangements by phone to get on the list.

e) Find out if it was possible to arrange for an appointment to get into

the embassy.

f) Get to the Cocodey clinic by 7:00 a.m.

g) Get to the French Embassy by 7:30 a.m.

Rachel looked through the phone book for the French Embassy phone number. There were about nine numbers listed. She began to call them. Each number was busy. She tried steadily for half an hour. Then, Mani took over. After twenty minutes, he tired, and I took over. I also tried for twenty minutes and gave up. We had no choice but to get there as early as possible and try to get in.

Since we were unsuccessful getting through to the French Embassy, I called Air France to arrange the flight home to Israel. I was dumbfounded when the clerk told me that the earliest booking was three weeks away. I asked to be put on "standby." There were so many people on "standby" that the earliest standby list I could get on was two weeks away!

That night I was too distraught to participate in the evening gathering in Rachel's living room. I took Nesya and went to bed almost immediately after leaving my name to be put on the standby list. Rachel had been gracious enough to give us the use of her bedroom for the week of our stay. I felt bad about having to impose upon her again, but I was in no position to change my predicament. I lay in her bed and tried to sleep, but sleep evaded me. I was trying to comprehend what had happened at the airport and what would be my best plan of action to free us from the clutches of an invisible enemy. I mulled over in my mind the agenda we had laid out earlier. Was there anything we had not thought of? Food! I had run out of food! Where was I going to get kosher food?! I also needed to inform my family in Israel what had happened. Being in a different time-zone and due to the hour I was supposed to arrive, I could still contact them before they left to meet me at the airport. One more thing – I had to contact my employer and tell them that my return flight had been delayed.

With the morning schedule planned, my thoughts drifted to my personal life and my past goals and aspirations. I was a middle-aged African-American Jewish divorcee. I had lived in Israel for about 25 years. Upon my arrival to Israel, I spent a year and a half on kibbutz, and then I moved to Jerusalem to study para-medicine. I had worked in three of the major hospitals before I decided to re-train to be an English teacher. During my first year of study, I married an Israeli. Shortly after our marriage, he was injured in a work accident. The psychological trauma had an adverse effect on our marriage, and we decided to divorce. Though it was difficult, I managed to move forward towards a degree in

ESL/EFL and Hebrew Language. The combination of these two majors greatly enhanced my success as a teacher.

My life was fulfilling, but I also wanted to build a family of my own. At the age of 36, I approached the Child Welfare Board of Israel to look into the possibility of adopting a child. There, I was informed that my age significantly limited my being approved for any kind of adoption. The board did allow me to be a part of a preparatory program for child fostering. Eventually, the age limit for adopting was raised, but due to an inability to harness my chronological acceleration, I was still considered "too old." To this dilemma, another obstacle was added. If I wanted to apply for foreign adoption, I would have to go through a local non-profit organization. Each of these organizations dealt with three parts of the world – Europe, Asia, and Latin America. ***None of them dealt with Africa, which was my continent of choice.***

Finding the process in Israel prohibitive, I took two years leave of absence from my job with the Israel Ministry of Education. While in the U.S.A., I also applied to be an adoptive parent. The training program began with a course for foster-parenting. It delved into many issues that might play a role in parent-child relationships. The course forced the participants to think and re-think their request to become parents and to view it from various angles. After finishing the program, my name was put on a waiting list, and, so, I waited to be called. Every day, when I returned home, I listened to the messages on my answering machine, hoping there would be one from Child Services. Weeks went by. Months went by. Finally, I had schedule my return flight to Israel because my sabbatical was ending. That very day, when I returned home with my airline ticket, there was that long-awaited message. "Please, contact us. There is a baby girl whom you can adopt." I was stupefied by the timing. I called to get more information about the baby. She was called "Precious," and she was born on the anniversary of my father's death. My heart seemed to do somersaults in my chest. With not a minute to spare, I called the authorities in Israel to see about extending my sabbatical. My request was referred to higher authorities. Twenty-four hours later, I was told that my sabbatical could not be extended without jeopardizing my tenure. With sadness and disappointment, I returned to Israel in the original state in which I had left, childless.

So, here I was, a few years later, fulfilling my dream to be a mother, and at the same time, I was caught in a web of impediment. Sometimes, when you are in such extreme circumstances, you just have to reach deep down inside of you, to the core of your soul and find that special "something" which can help you cope with the situation. For me, it was an old Negro Spiritual, "The Lord Will Make a Way Somehow." With a song in my heart and a prayer on my lips, I fell asleep.

The next morning we arrived at the embassy at 7:30 a.m. To our surprise, the crowd was almost as large as it was the previous day. However, this time, we had enough food and drink to last us for the day. Today's "activity" was pretty much a repeat of the day before. Again, we tried to get the guard to reveal to us how to get on the list, but he would not divulge a thing. We asked him to add our names to the list, and he pretended he did not hear us. For some reason, his disposition reminded me of Idi Amin, and this stirred inside me a capricious desire to do something bizarre, like beating my chest and roaring like King Kong. I had to restrain myself from doing anything that would be detrimental to my goal (i.e. getting a visa for my daughter). Having made no progress, except to move a few meters forward, towards the embassy compound, at noon we decided to leave and to try our luck the next day. Back at the "consulate," the nickname we had given to Rachel's flat, we discussed ways to surmount this hurdle. We tried futilely to get through by telephone to the French Embassy.

On the third day, I went straight up to the guard and said, "Help me." This was the first time he looked directly at us. He asked me my name. He wrote it and Nesya's name at the bottom of the list. There were still 50 names ahead of ours when the gate was closed for the day.

On the fourth day, I stood directly in front of him and asked for the phone number to call to get on the list. He tore off a scrap of paper and wrote the number. Dora and Mani ran to the "phone booth" across the street and handed the "clerk" the number. Of course, when the person tried to call the number, the line was busy. That is the way it stayed for the rest of the time they stood there. Keeping eye-contact with them, I approached the guard. I did not ask him to put our names on the list; I just said our names, and he wrote them down.

On the fifth day, (Friday), the guard automatically wrote our names on the list. At 11:15 a.m., he motioned for us to go into the fenced-off area outside of the compound. Our bags and passports were examined, but we were not allowed to enter the compound. We were number 192. At the front of the line, there was a glass door, which we would have to pass through to enter the compound. I counted about 27 people between me and that door. At about 11:22, a guard stepped in front of the glass door and called numbers 165 to 173. After "number 173" stepped inside, he shut the door behind him. At 11:36, numbers 174 through 181 were called. Almost in unison, the rest of us stepped forward, like soldiers reporting for duty. There were now 11 people in front of me. My optimism rose. At 11:51, numbers 182 to 191 were called. I stood as close to the glass door as possible, awaiting my turn. I looked back for the first time and noticed that there were about 100 people in line behind me. At exactly 12 noon, the guard opened the door, and several applicants walked out. I stepped forward to go in, and the guard said," Sorry, we're closed!" I was so shocked, I could not move. People behind me began to shout. One woman screamed and slumped to the ground. She wailed, cried, and thrashed, as if she was having an epileptic seizure. She mumbled, almost incoherently, that she had been trying for so long to get a visa, how hard she had been trying to get inside the compound, and how she could no longer take the humiliation and disgrace. A strong feeling of empathy lurched inside me, and it almost propelled me to join her in a display of desperation. It took a lot of internal will to prevent me from making a spectacle of myself. Someone gave her water and tried to comfort her. As if under the spell of this woman's "fit," the crowd moved forward as if to storm the embassy. Guards appeared out of nowhere. They surrounded us and herded us like cattle, out of the courtyard. The ordeal was traumatic. I felt that I really had to gird myself in order not to breakdown, like that unfortunate woman. I could not think. My body was propelling itself as if on remote control, as if it were physically attached to the larger body of people being herded out to the compound. This larger body mass was throbbing with pain and was stunned by the total lack of sensitivity shown by the "master" in charge. Our destiny was completely at its whims and mercy.

When I met Mani and Dora outside the compound, they didn't ask questions. I am sure that the tortured look on my face said it all. Dora took Nesya from my arms, which were painfully frozen in the position they had been in from holding Nesya for hours. We flagged down a taxi to take us to the Cocodey clinic for Nesya's second injection of the day. On the way, I told them what had happened at the embassy. They were silent. In all our minds was the thought that we must try to take care of the immediate concerns, such as Nesya's injection and getting additional medication for her. Dr. Quanton wanted to start giving Nesya vitamin supplements. These vitamins could only be obtained at one pharmacy that was located on the opposite side of the Riveria Place neighborhood. We had less than one hour to get from the clinic to the pharmacy, and then to Rachel's in time for me to prepare for the Sabbath. To save time, we ask the taxi driver to wait for us when we arrived at the pharmacy. He was more than happy to do so.

By the time we arrived at Rachel's, I had about 20 minutes to prepare for the Sabbath. Fortunately (or unfortunately), I didn't have much food to prepare. My meals consisted of matza, canned corn, sardines, and yogurts. I lit candles on the windowsill overlooking the lagoon of Abidjan. For a moment, I paused and tried to imagine that I was back in Israel. How I yearned to be back in my home in Israel, welcoming in the Shabbat. I held Nesya close to me, trying to infuse in her the spirit of Shabbat. In order to extend this feeling of tranquility, I sat in a chair in the corner near the window. I needed to move into a different time-frame. I needed to relax and forget the day's woes. Nesya sat quietly on my lap, entwining her fingers in mine and looking for clues from me what we would do next. I wanted to do absolutely **nothing,** particularly, not to think about anything. The sunrays, shining through the far end of the red tapestry curtains, softened the glow of the setting sun. Then, I knew that Shabbat had fully arrived. In order to "daven" (i.e. "pray") in privacy, I took Nesya with me to our little bedroom next to Rachel's bedroom. (I had insisted that Rachel move back into her room.) Often, when we pray the same prayers daily, we are not able to sustain a deep level of intention. However, this Sabbath I felt in tune with every word. Words that I had hardly noticed before took on a newer, deeper meaning. Two Psalms that are included in the Sabbath eve prayers stirred in me very strong emotions- Psalms 92 and Psalms 100:

Psalms 92

A Song for the Sabbath day.

It is a good thing to give thanks unto the L-rd,

and to sing praises unto Your name, O most High,

To show forth Your loving kindness in the morning,

And Your faithfulness every night.

Upon an instrument of ten strings and upon the psaltery,

Upon the harp with a solemn sound.

The righteous shall flourish like the palm tree;

He shall grow like a cedar in Levanon.

Those that be planted in the house of the L-rd

Shall flourish in the courts of our G-d.

They shall bring forth fruit in old age . . .

Psalms 100

A Psalm of Thanksgiving

Make a joyful noise unto the L-rd, all ye lands.

Serve the L-rd with gladness

Come before His presence with singing.

Know ye that the L-rd, He is G-d.

It is He who has made us,

And we belong to Him;

We are His people, and the sheep of His pasture.

Enter into His gates with thanksgiving

And into His courts with praise.

Be thankful unto Him, and bless His name.

For the L-rd is good; His mercy is everlasting,

And His truth endureth to all generations.

The residents of the house respected my Sabbath observance and admired the portion of the table which I had set for the Shabbat meal. I used my last bit of grape juice for "Kiddush," and I was saddened by the thought that there would be none left for "Havdala" (the short prayer service at the conclusion of the Sabbath). After the ritual handwashing, I made the blessing for the bread (i.e. the matza). As I placed a bite-size piece in my mouth, I thought about the significance of matza. Matza is the bread of affliction, the bread of poverty, but it is also a symbol of leaving slavery and moving into freedom. Though I was not in slavery, I surely was not in a state of freedom. I was stranded in Africa against my will. I had no idea when or how I would leave and return to Israel. The Jewish people has been through many trials and tribulations, but G-d has never forsaken us. I had no doubt that He would deliver us. In all ways we must acknowledge Him, and He will direct our paths. His faithfulness has been with us through all generations, from Avraham, our patriarch, until today. When we were in Egypt, we had matza. Even in Theresienstadt, during the Holocaust in Europe, Jews found a way to secretly bake matza. Though their bodies were enslaved, their minds were free. They knew that no situation is permanent. Six million Jews were killed in World War II. Six hundred thousand were in Israel when statehood was declared in 1948. This is the same number of Israelites who left Egypt. We/I shall overcome!

This thought stayed with me for the rest of the Sabbath. I enjoyed the freedom of being able to sit with Nesya on the veranda and look at the children playing on the grassy or sandy knolls. There was only one area that was officially designated as a children's play area, and there was only one "jungle-gym" which all the children had to share. I was amazed that there were no fights over it. The youngsters took turns politely. I enjoyed looking at Nesya's bright smile as she climbed up on my lap. I enjoyed hearing her say, "Maman," the French equivalent of "Mommy." I enjoyed the freedom of not worrying about what the next day would entail. I enjoyed the inner peace I felt, knowing that G-d would not forsake me.

And thus, was the evening and the morning of the seventh day.

. . . .

On Sunday, I was pretty much left alone. The residents at the "ULE," donned their best clothes and went to church. I took Nesya out for a walk. I was afraid to venture far because I did not know French, and I was afraid I would get lost. About three blocks away was a shopping center – or what was left of a shopping center. This area had been targeted in the last coup d'etat, and most of the stores and been pillaged and burnt. Now, all except three stores- the supermarket, a bookstore, and a travel agency- the rest were boarded-up, but the stones above the window frames, scorched black from the torchings, were still an eery testimony of what had transpired.

My first destination, when I took Nesya out for a walk was to go into the supermarket to try to find something with a kosher symbol. I had already been warned not to eat fresh fruits and vegetables because of the irrigation sanitation – or lack of it. This was difficult for me. I loved fruits and vegetables, and the ones in the supermarket were large and beautiful. There were fruits which I had never seen, and I really wanted to try them. I knew I would be taking a chance if I did; so I had to forgo this luxury.

I examined every can of fruit, every can of corn or peas and the like. I read all the fine print on the tins of sardines. I checked the peanut butter labels. Nothing had any semblance of Kashrut. Once, when Dora, Rachel, and Mani came with me to the store, everyone one of them helped me check the products. At one point, Mani came running over to me, shouting, "I found something! I found something!" I was so excited, but when I checked what he thought was a kosher symbol, I discovered that it was only a "Registered" symbol. What a disappointment! In order not to starve to death, I knew I would have to resort to relying on cans of vegetables whose ingredients were cooked only with water and salt. Sardines, which had been prepared in 100% vegetable oil, I also added to my diet, but these sardines were not always available. Canned fruit cooked in sugar syrup expanded my meager diet. Dairy products were another problem, which I was not sure how to deal with; so I bought yogurts for Nesya, but I would not eat them myself. Bread, however, was the biggest problem. Baguettes were very popular, probably because of the French influence. There was a bakery at the back of the supermarket. Fresh bread was baked there daily. The smell of fresh bread was most enticing, but not enticing enough for me to try it. At least I could smell it without "treifing-up" my body.

Besides trying to find food suitable for me to eat, going to the supermarket had become a social event. There were many foreigners, either attached to their local embassies or international businesses. I met people from all over the world. I even met a few Americans, some of whom had married Africans. We often chatted while standing in the check-out line. No one ever suggested exchanging phone numbers or addresses. So my social outings consisted of making small-talk in the supermarket queue. When it was my turn to check-out, I noticed how similar the courtesy was to that of the United States. Also, there was a check-out boy who bagged the groceries for the customers. There was one difference, if he asked if you needed help carrying the groceries out of the store or to your car, you were expected to "tip" him. I was lucky that Rachel had accompanied me on my first excursion, or I might have found myself in an embarrassing situation.

The cashiers and the check-out boys had come to recognize me. They always greeted me politely. I was already brave enough to say, "Bonjour." However, when it came to paying for my groceries, I just handed them all my money like a four-year-old child having her first experience in "handling business." Inflation was so bad there and the value of the local Franc was so low, compared to foreign currency, that every time I bought the smallest amount of items, they always cost more than 1,000 C.I. Francs. I had no idea how much things cost or how much I was spending. Of course, I never counted my change; I just balled it up and stuck it in my billfold.

After leaving the supermarket, I would walk across the pavement to the bookstore. Most of the books in the windows were in French. Some were in German. Very few, if any, were in English. I tried to read the titles of the books.

Some, I actually understand. There were very cute children's books. Inside the store, I tried to entertain Nesya by showing her the children's books. She seemed to enjoy this. Since I always carried her in a baby-carriage backpack, she became very heavy, in spite of her tiny size. So I would often have to end my outing long before I had wanted to. I would walk across the parking lot, cross the main street, and meander among the street vendors on the opposite side of the road. After I turned off the main road, the walking became more difficult because the "sidewalks" were not completely paved, and I would have to plough my way through sand and dirt – and with Nesya on my back and groceries in my arms. Near the Riveria Place complex were newspaper stands and street "phone booths" like those near the French Embassy. I would glance at the newspapers to try to decipher what was currently happening in the Ivory Coast. My attempts were not very fruitful. I could not pick-up on the atmosphere in the country. I knew there had to be some concern about the political and military situation in the country, but I was not sure how much of this had filtered down to the local residents.

Once back at Rachel's apartment building, I still had to climb the five flights of stairs. By the time I reached the flat, I was totally exhausted. I put my groceries away and took Nesya to sit on the veranda so that she could watch the children playing, while she ate her yogurt. Shortly after we returned from our little outing, the residents of ULE returned. They had a festive meal and sat around singing hymns. After the Sunday meal and singing was over, everyone sat around watching television. I was not sure why they bothered to watch; the programs repeated themselves every few hours, especially on Sundays. Most of the Sunday programs consisted of church choirs singing. For some reason the singers seemed to think that their singing would be enhanced if they waved colored silk scarves while swaying in time with the music. The words of the songs might have been different, but the style of singing was always the same. The one thing that I did notice was how indigenous the African flavor was in African-American melodies. Africans did not sing gospels, but the rich harmony that permeated each song was comforting to the soul. However, after a few hours of this "comfort", I was saturated, and I needed a rest from the "balm in Gilead." So, I sat on the porch with Nesya, waiting for that moment when a cool, less humid breeze would blow across the knolls and up to the apartments. By now, it was nearly dark outside; so, I prepared myself for the next day, which meant going back to the French Embassy.

So, the next morning, we (the four of us) found ourselves, standing in the crowd outside the French Embassy. I am not sure whether it was because the guard had pity on me or whether he just got tired of seeing my face, he allowed me to cross the barrier and stand at the beginning of the line. Whatever the reason, on my ninth trip to the embassy, the guard looked at his list and motioned for me to go in. By eleven o'clock, I was inside, filling out forms, paying registration fees, and having my documents checked. The forms were dutifully stamped and attached to Nesya's passport. Then, I was told, "Come back this afternoon at four o'clock." Though I was wary that there would be some "hitch" on the way, I was stunned at the fact that, though it seemed that her passport had been stamped, it could not be given to me immediately.

I carried Nesya outside and showed Dora and Mani the receipt with which to reclaim Nesya's passport. We had to decide what to do for the next four hours. If we drove back to Riveria Place, by the time we got there, it would almost be time to turn around and come back. If we stayed in town for these four hours, we would be exhausted by the heat. We decided to head back to Riveria Place and rest for a half an hour.

On the way back to the French Embassy, I was filled with apprehension. We arrived at 3:30 p.m. There was *no one* in sight – not even a guard! The compound seemed totally deserted. We walked along the outside wall, trying to find someone who might know what was happening. However, no "official-looking" person was in sight. People began to appear, people who evidently hoped to receive their visas. All of them seemed to know where to go. At the extreme end of the compound, at the end of a dirt brick wall, there was a dilapidated fence, in the middle of which was an equally dilapidated gate. Everyone congregated around this gate. At four o'clock, there still was no sign of activity inside the embassy. At 4:30 p.m., someone appeared outside the embassy building, but he was not even looking in the direction of the gate. Then, he disappeared and was never seen again. At 4:45, people began to crowd around the gate. A local fellow came over to me and offered his services. I was not sure if what he was telling me was the truth, but I felt the need to trust him. He explained to me that as soon as the iron gate opened, people would stampede across the vacant parking lot and fight for a place in line that would allow them to receive a number, which was necessary to enter the embassy. Without this number, I would have to return the next day – and the next day – until I managed to be close enough to the beginning of the line in order to get a number.

. . . . . And, thus, it was. When the indifferent clerk, finally, strolled over to open the gate, pandemonium broke out, as people tried to jockey to be the first ones to enter. People were knocked down in the process. I saw eyeglasses flying through the air and several people knocked to the ground. The clerk hardly had time to jump aside as the people plowed through like a herd of wild bulls. I looked around for "my young man" and found him standing ***right*** beside the ticket-giver. I stayed "in line," and he casually strolled over to me and handed me a ticket that had the number eleven written on it. This made certain that I would be able to enter the embassy and get the precious visa. I paid the young fellow $50 for this privilege.

Once inside the embassy, the numbers we had received seemed to be of no further value. We were shifted around, from station to station, according to a system that only an insider could understand. By some "mini-miracle," I got to the right station, and the clerk pulled out Nesya's passport from a stack of other passports. Before leaving the embassy, I checked to be sure that the long awaited visa had really been obtained. Yes! There it was! Then, I noticed that the visa was a temporary visa, valid for only two weeks – and I didn't even have a secured flight reservation!

Since I had arrived in Abidjan, rumors of a pending coup d'état were rampant. Most foreigners were trying every route possible to leave the Ivory Coast. All flights were fully booked for at least the next two months, depending on the desirability of the airline. In most cases, when I tried to book a flight, I could not even get on a "stand-by" list. Whenever I was able, I kept my name on that list and applied again two days later, to get on another stand-by list. I had to maximize my chances of getting on a flight. In the three weeks I had been there, I had never been scheduled for a flight. The thought struck me like a thunderbolt – **_what if I was not able to obtain a flight reservation before the two weeks were up!_** I would have to repeat this torture of trying to get a visa.

What should have been a time of elation turned into a point of major worry. What if . . . . I knew I had to develop a back-up plan. As soon as we arrived at ULE, we had a "consul" meeting. First of all, we made of list of things we needed to do so that we could best utilize our time and effort. We knew we had to try as many embassies and consulates as possible to see what were their visa requirements. At the same time, we had to be sure that these countries had airline service from Abidjan. We also had to find out if there was a connecting flight to Israel. We prepared an organized chart:

EMBASSIES:	COUNTRIES' AIRLINES:
Phone Number:	Phone Number:
Address:	Address:

QUESTIONS FOR EMBASSIES:

1) Does the country require visas for stays less than a month?
2) What ages must have a visa?
3) What are the requirements for obtaining a visa?
4) How long does it take to process the forms and obtain a visa?
5) Can we make an appointment to go to the embassy?

QUESTIONS FOR AIRLINES:

1) Does your airline have flights directly to Israel?
2) Does your airline have a stop in another country where I can get a connecting flight to Israel?
3) At what hours are there flights from Abidjan to countries which have connecting flights?
4) Is it possible to book a reservation now?
5) If there is a stand-by list, is it possible to reserve a place on the stand-by list?
6) What number will we be on the stand-by list?
7) If there is no room on the stand-by list, is there a waiting list for the stand-by list?

During the next week, we became "experts" on rules and regulations for foreign visas. After having called more than 10 embassies, consulates and about 15 airlines, we narrowed the possibilities down to seven countries and four airlines. Then, we had to plan a schedule for going to the embassies. We decided that it was best to scheduled appointments according to embassies in close proximity. Therefore, we had to check the city maps in the phone directory to find out their locations. My head was spinning and my nerves were frayed from dealing with such tedious detail, but it had to be done in the most efficient manner if we were to succeed. We had to make out a very precise worksheet of co-ordination between embassies/consulates and airline service offered. Then, we would have to call each office to obtain the necessary information, and afterwards, we would have to decide if it was at all feasible to continue the pursuit. The airline service was just as critical to our success as the visa requirements. Though there were at least 15 countries which had consulates or embassies in Abidjan, few of them had airlines which flew directly there. It was useless to book a flight with an airline which would require several stopovers in countries for which a visa might be required. Many of the airlines, which had service to and from Abidjan, were airlines I had never heard of, and many had stopovers in Moslem countries. Except for the American and French embassies, which were adjacent to each other, most of the other embassies were scattered throughout the city. That meant that only if we managed to get to one embassy early enough, we could try to get to a second embassy before it closed for the morning. If not, we would have a four-hour wait until the embassy re-opened in the afternoon. The two most promising embassies were the

Dutch and the Swiss. Because of its approximate location to the Air France office, we decided to approach the American Embassy first, and then the Swiss Embassy. Later, if needed, we would apply to the Dutch Embassy. The American Embassy was less desirable because this meant that I would have to apply for international adoption recognition and fly to the States in order to return to Israel. However, I could not ignore any possibility.

Chapter Four

The U.S. Embassy

Often Americans think that their citizenship and passport are a certificate which will protect them wherever they travel. They are shocked and appalled when non-Americans treat them with disdain or have the audacity to insult their homeland and abuse them physically. I was fully aware that carrying an American passport could be a curse or a blessing. I had a two-fold purpose in approaching the U.S. Embassy in Abidjan. First of all, I had to register with them because of the pending coup d'etat. It might help if foreign nationals would be evacuated by their embassies. Secondly, I wanted to try to get a visa to take my daughter to the States if I was unable to obtain a visa to return with her to Israel.

I started my daily routine of arising just in time to see the sunrise. I stood by the window near the balcony and watched the first rays of light appearing as a backdrop over the black lagoon. Then, the mist parted as a gauze curtain ushering in today's play. I said my morning prayers seriously, trying to clear the air and the atmosphere of the prayer service that the devout Christians had held at three that morning, beseeching their god to save my soul. I prayed to have strength to hold up through the unending ordeal which I was facing. I prayed for wisdom to make the right decisions and find the right people who could help me. The words of Kalev ben Yefuneh (when he heard the fearful tales of the spies before entering Jericho) blazed their way into my mind. "We shall overcome!" These words were my anchor for the rest of the day.

The sky had become a misty grey-purple. I knew it was time for me to prepare breakfast and lunch for the day. As I approached the kitchen, I stood for a moment to listen for the scurrying of the last rats outside the screen protected shutters. Though we were on the fifth floor, huge rats scurried from early evening until early morning, up and down the walls just outside the kitchen windows and balcony, trying to bite a hole that would allow them to crawl through the screen into the kitchen. Every now and then, I would get a glimpse of one. They were as big as cats, and they bared their teeth in anger at having their freedom of movement limited.

The first thing I did was put two pots of water on the fire to boil; one was small – for Nesya's porridge and the other one was large – for the first of our two daily baths. The boiler had broken ages ago, and there was no money to repair it; so, each of the 9-13 occupants had to heat water daily for baths or take cold showers. While the water was heating, I checked to see if the clothes, which I had hand-washed and had hung on the balcony, had dried. The humidity in Abidjan was always about 90%, and often it took three days for the clothes to dry. With so many people in the apartment, the clothes were hung in layers, freshly washed clothes put underneath the drier ones. I peered down at the grassy knoll in the courtyard. It, too, was covered with clothing spread out to dry. I found a skirt for myself and a dress for Nesya, both of which were just damp enough to iron dry. I plugged in the iron and placed the clothes on the table (i.e. ironing board) on the kitchen balcony. I fought my way through the clothes which hung from clothes lines strung the length of the kitchen pantry. I jumped when I heard the scurrying of a rat, running along the shutters. I noticed a new larger hole in the screen. I worried that the next morning I would find a rat in the kitchen. I ironed the clothes as best I could, with the iron that didn't work properly and a table that shook while I tried to iron. The, I saw Mani, standing in the doorway, fingering his shirt to see if it could be ironed dry. I took it from him and ironed it, while he prepared our food basket for the day.

Nesya began to stir. Mani went to pick her up. She rested her head on his chest, but when she saw me, she reached out for me. I needed her show of affection. I gathered up our clothes but did not unplug the iron. There were already two more people waiting to iron their clothes. I took Nesya into my arms, patted her diaper to see how wet it was and then took her to the bedroom in order to change it. I did the ritual washing of her little hands. I sat her in the high-chair and looked at it and at her for a minute. From its appearance, it could have been the high-chair I had had when I was a baby. It was wooden and had several layers of white paint that had chipped and had been painted over. Its food tray had a familiar squeak, when raised or lowered. I looked at Nesya's nearly bald head. I, too, had had very little hair as a baby, and the neighborhood children had made up a chant to tease me about it. I smiled a lot as a baby, and now so did she. Rachel called me to warn me that the cream of wheat was about to boil over. I hurried to the kitchen to turn off the fire and stir it. Managing in the kitchen was still awkward for me, not only because of trying to keep kosher, but also because of the way things were done. I poured the cream of wheat into a bowl, added powdered baby formula to it and a pinch of sugar. Nesya had a ferocious appetite. She ate all the cereal and wanted more. I gave her a yogurt instead because I wanted to get ready to leave as soon as possible.

The bathing water was still not quite hot enough, but there was no time to wait. We needed to empty the pot and refill it for the next person. I poured part of the lukewarm water into the blue laundry tub and added just a little tap water to stretch it for two baths and so that it would not be too cool. I bathed Nesya first. Her spindly arms held on to the rim of the tub. I applied the special anti-bacterial soap to her skin which was badly scarred from festering mosquito bites. Then, I wrapped a towel around her and carried her to the bedroom. After I had dried her, I applied another anti-bacterial cream to her skin. Following this, I put baby powder around her neck and in her diaper before I fastened it. I dressed her in the blue denim dress which I had just ironed. Dora came to take her to "do" her hair. Nesya's hair was less than a half-inch long in the few places she had hair, but Dora was amazing in what she could do with it. She pulled it and tied it with multi-colored rubber bands. She found the biggest ribbon possible to tie on top to help soften her look and to emphasize that she is a girl. The bows never stayed on for the whole day, but it was a nice try. It was now my turn to bathe. I poured the rest of the water into the blue tub, and I took the pot back to the kitchen for the next person to use. I scrubbed the night's sweat off of me. I used the most perfumed liquid soap that I could find, because I knew that, shortly, I would be perspiring profusely. The bathroom and, especially, the bedroom smelled musty, even though they were cleaned daily. They were always a little damp from humidity which bred a rank odor. I poured the tepid water all over my body, as I stood in the blue pail. I tried to capture the feeling of a real shower. As soon as I dried myself and began to dress, I began to feel the first beads of sweat on my shoulders and arms. I generously sprinkled talcum powder inside my clothing to absorb the layer of moisture that was collecting inside. I applied a scant amount of make-up, glanced at myself in a mirror and went to the living room where Mani, Nesya, and Dora were waiting for me. Nesya held out her arms for me to pick her up. I held her high and then we rubbed noses, which had become our custom. Dora helped me adjust Nesya in the baby-carrier/backpack. "Ciao" we said to the others who were getting ready to start their day. Each one blessed us, in their own way and said they would be looking forward to hearing good news when we returned.

The dark stairwell had become familiar to me and I descended without fear of missing a step and falling. I walked down the stairs with a bounce, and Nesya giggled. We stood at the curb, waiting for a taxi, then climbed in and told the driver to head for downtown. This had become a daily routine. Nesya immediately fell asleep. If my situation had not been so desperate, I could have enjoyed these rides through the Ivory Coast countryside. Now, I could only think about my day's mission.

In order to get to the US Embassy, the driver took the same route that passed the French Embassy. On the way, I noticed a sign which said "Palm Beach Hotel", where I had originally planned to stay. I wondered what it was like inside and what I would have done alone with Nesya when I had arrived. The thought made me shiver. Would Nesya have survived if I had been alone with her in a hotel, not knowing that she was desperately ill and on the verge of death? I blotted the thought out of my mind and gently rubbed her little head.

The line, in front of the U. S. Embassy, was almost as long as the ones in front of the French Embassy. There were huge stone barriers that prevented vehicle and pedestrian access to the building. Once passed these barriers, there were several different lines, and only those familiar with the routine knew which line to stand in. The guard at the first check point was a local. He, intentionally or unintentionally, was unhelpful. We got in different lines; we had learned this from the long waits at the French Embassy. We stood for about twenty minutes, while people were again questioned, their hand bags and briefcases searched, and a body scanner was run along their body. Finally, it was my turn to be checked. I showed the guard my American passport. He looked at me, at my passport picture, and at me again. Then, he told me, "You are in the wrong line. Go to the line over there." This was the line that Dora was standing in. I pushed my way through the crowd and stood at her side. She gave a little sigh, indicating how much she hated the local bureaucracy. I had resigned myself to the fact that things like this were going to happen and tried not to let myself get worked up about it. Still, a depressive mood, which seemed to prevail around me, settled into its usual position, just outside my aura. This was my signal to be prepared for anything to happen and to burrow in for the challenge. I motioned for Mani to join us. When it was our turn, the guard looked at Dora's passport and pointed to a line on the porch along the side of the Embassy building.

"Get in the line over there." Mani, who was carrying Nesya, stepped forward and handed the guard their passport. The guard scrutinized them and said, "You cannot go any further." We looked at each other in disbelief. I stepped forward and said, "But we are all together, and that's my baby!" This guard, also a local national, looked totally confused. Since he had to maintain his position of authority, he said, "You can go inside, but they will have to wait here!", and he pointed to several benches near the guard post. I felt the urge to scream, but controlled myself. I looked around for an American official in uniform. Standing at the head of another line was a soldier in army uniform. I didn't bother to get in line and walked directly over to him. Those in line gave me a look of disapproval. I stuck my passport in his face and said, "I am an American citizen. That is my newly adopted baby over there, and the two people with her are her caretakers. They need to go inside with me." The soldier checked my passport, picked up some kind of communication device, spoke into it and looked towards the entrance of the Embassy. The door opened and a soldier in Marine uniform came out and walked towards us. The guard pointed to me and said, "See if you can help her." I repeated my story. The Marine asked to see my passport. After looking through it, he gestured towards me with a polite bow and said, "Please." Then, he walked towards Mani, Dora and Nesya. He checked their passports and told us to follow him. We followed him up the steps to a porch outside the building. He instructed Mani and Dora to wait outside and told me to go inside and get a number. Before I could get a number, my personal belongings were checked again and then I had to place them on a conveyor belt which transported them through a scanning machine.

During this procedure, I was questioned about my place of birth, my residency, my profession, what my purpose was for being in the Ivory Coast, and what my reason was for coming to the Embassy. The process was slow and tedious. The number I got was 98. I asked those in the anteroom what numbers they had. Number 56 was the lowest number. The Embassy had opened at 9 a.m. It was now 11 a.m. Fifty-five people had had their papers processed in two hours. That meant that I had about a two hour wait before I could get into the inner office to have mine processed. I went outside to inform the others what the situation was. We all sighed simultaneously. "It's a good thing we brought extra food with us today," said Dora. ". . . and extra diapers," added Mani. Nesya was hungry and wet. At the far end of the building was another door. People were entering and exiting freely. Mani decided to explore the area. He returned with a smile of his face. It was a small room with a couple of vending machines and bathrooms! This was good news to all of us. Dora found a place to change Nesya's diaper. I sat on a bench outside and set out the food for our lunch. It consisted mainly of fruit and yogurts and crackers. Mani decided to buy something from one of the vending machines. Fortunately, he had a few U.S. dollars with him.

While we were having lunch, I looked through the forms I had to fill-out. I began to worry. The price for processing the papers was $45, with the words "exact sum" underlined. I had $50 travelers checks. The Embassy had no place to change money, which meant that we would have to leave the Embassy compound in order to change money. Another problem was the required passport pictures for

Nesya. From previous experience, I knew that the U.S. government was very strict in its requirements for passport pictures. Mani said that he had the negatives of her passport pictures and while I was waiting, he could go and have pictures made. He gulped down his sandwich and headed out – Dora with him, in order to translate. In the meantime, I tried to find ways to entertain Nesya. We walked up and down the veranda, looking at the flowers. Then, we noticed a grey-brown lizard, hiding underneath the steps. He did not seem to be afraid of us; he just stared at us. Nesya pointed at him and babbled something. When she tried to touch him, he scampered away.

More than an hour had passed, and Dora and Mani had not returned. Nesya was becoming restless. We had walked the length of the veranda probably 50 times. It was hot, and the lizards must have been having a siesta under the porch, because not one had poked its head out for a long time. Every childhood game that I could remember had been played again and again. Usually, at this hour Nesya would have fallen asleep. For some reason, today, she was wide awake. When I held her and tried to rock her to sleep, she fidgeted and climbed off my lap. She would grab my hand and pull me to get up. Again, we would walk the length of the porch. My legs were beginning to ache. Almost all the people who had been waiting on the veranda with us had entered the Embassy, had their papers processed and left. A few new people came to join us. A couple with a child about Nesya's age came and sat on the bench next to us. Nesya and the little boy played hide and seek under the bench. They held hands and tried to walk down the steps, nearly toppling over as they did. Each struggled to try to help the other one up. Both of them were on "all four", arms and legs entangled and Pamper-padded rear-ins stuck up in the air. The boy's father went over to help them untangle themselves. As soon as they were up-righted, they grabbed each other's hand and headed off again, looking for something else to explore. I was glad for the temporary distraction, but soon my thoughts were drawn back to the fact that Mani and Dora had not returned. I looked up at the large black framed oval clock hanging on the wall at the far end of the veranda. It was now 11:40 in the morning.

While I was still gazing at the clock, I heard someone calling me. It was Mani, running towards the Embassy check-point, waving an envelope. "I've got them!" he shouted. I scooped up Nesya and ran out to meet him. I explained to the guard that they were returning with the passport pictures I needed to process my papers. I thrust Nesya into Dora's arms and rushed towards the doorway of the Embassy so that I could go through the meticulous security check again. I had to leave all my personal items (except my passport and billfold) at the desk. I was given a laminated number in order to claim them later.

After clearing the security check in the anteroom, I was instructed to follow the corridor to the end and turn left. On the way, I noticed several smaller rooms where foreign nationals were being questioned, each trying to come-up with the right answers to obtain that precious piece of paper stamped "Visa." The room where I had to wait was so small that there was only room for one armchair, and a two-seat sofa. The only other piece of furniture was a folding chair, crammed against the wall, underneath the ledge of the bullet-proof window, behind which the embassy workers stood to accept applications. All seats were occupied; so, I had to stand. Standing for 40 minutes in such cramped quarters made my legs ache. I shifted my weight from one foot to the other, trying to relieve the pain. Finally, I asked one of the men sitting on the love-seat if he would mind if I sat on the armrest. Since the age of feminism, men were less prone to get up for women, for fear of having a barrage of insults hurled at them. After sitting in this fashion for 10 minutes, my legs became numb; so, I stood up again. Finally, one of the applicants was called to the counter, and with swift brazenness, I jumped into his seat. Ten minutes later, I was called to the window for the clerk to review my forms. I paid the fee with the money Mani had brought back from cashing my traveler's check on the black market. (In order to cash it legally in a bank, I would have had to go to the bank myself. This would have wasted valuable time.) After the clerk gave me my receipt, he asked for the form with the passport pictures. He read through it carefully, writing comments on the side. He put a check in the appropriate boxes in the section at the bottom, marked "Official Use Only." When he removed Nesya's passport pictures from the envelope, he looked at them and said, "These pictures are unacceptable. You'll have to get new ones." Then, he handed me a slip of paper with the names and addresses of local photo shops, which were approved by the US Embassy. I asked the clerk which one was the nearest and how long it would take to get there. He said all three were within walking distance, but the closest one was 10 minutes away. He warned me that the shop would close at 1 p.m; so, I had better hurry.

Fortunately, leaving the Embassy compound was less time-consuming than entering it. I handed in the plastic number that I had received, grabbed my things and dashed outside. I babbled almost incoherently to Mani and Dora, trying to explain as quickly as possible what we had to do in less than 15 minutes. Nesya had fallen asleep. Dora and Mani slid her into the baby-carrier and put it on my back. As we were hurrying by the check-in guard, I shouted to him that we had to go get new passport pictures. We walked as fast as we could, but the sidewalks were broken and only partially paved. We had to walk in the street part of the way. I kept sinking into the red sandy dirt as I walked, and this impeded my progress. Mani put the backpack on his back. By the time we got to the street where the photo shop was located, his face and white shirt were soaked with sweat. We were on a midtown city street with people meandering along. We had to maneuver between them and, at the same time, keep our pace. We looked for the sign of the photo shop and tried to find building numbers as we hurried along. Finally, as we approached the end of the street, we saw a sign hanging at the corner, almost underneath the traffic light. In large red letters on a yellow background, was written "Photo Shop." In smaller black letters, near the bottom of the sign, was written "U.S. passport pictures." Because Dora was taller than us, she sprinted ahead to make the 1 p.m. headline. However, it was now 1:02 p.m. The shop owner apologized and said that he could not help us because we were late. He told us we would have to return at 2:15 p.m. We all began to shout at him in our native tongues – I, in English; Dora in French; and Mani in Pele. The shopkeeper's eyes grew large, but he stood his ground while ushering us outside. He locked the door and

77

walked away. We stood there, looking at his back as he strolled away. Dora gritted her teeth and let out a scream, not typical to her usual composure.

Nesya, who had been sleeping, woke up and began to cry. She was wet and hungry. I was wondering how we were going to manage with her for the rest of the day. Outside the photo shop, on the edge of the sidewalk, near the curb, was a row of benches. Men were sitting and playing a type of backgammon and having lunch. One noticed us standing there and saw Nesya crying. He told the others to move over so that we could sit down. The green slats of the benches were extremely uncomfortable and sticky. I could not bear to sit on them. Dora sat and fed Nesya a yogurt, the last of our food supply. All of us were exhausted and hungry. Local vendors were selling cooked meat that looked like "kebab." Mani wanted to buy something to eat. Dora advised against it, for sanitary reasons. Mani walked up and down the street until he found a vendor which looked somewhat clean. Dora bought packaged cheese crackers. I had nothing.

Though it was hot, we decided to explore the local open-air market. As we walked along, Mani saw some shops which caught his fancy. There was a shop which sold cameras, stereos, and music discs. Then he found an upscale men's clothing store. At the end of the street, urban Abidjan seemed to transform into a village market. Except for the language spoken, I could have been standing outside the Nablus Gate of the Old City of Jerusalem. Some vendors, selling tormus, even had the green, blue and red push-carts used in the marketplace of Jerusalem's Old City. Along the curb were stalls selling new and used shoes, tourist T-shirts, and jade figurines. Some stalls bore a wide assortment of newspapers, magazines, and trashy paperback books. We pushed our way along the crowded sidewalk, where the vendors hawked their wares. At one point, we came upon some steps that led to an underground market. It almost looked like a path to hell, and I was afraid to enter. However, trying to overcome my fears, I gingerly stepped down on the first step.

Once inside it was less frightening than it had originally seemed. The path from the steps led to the fruit and vegetables section. Further along was a men's clothing section. Then, the path led to a "kitchenware" section, which mainly sold grinding tools for pulverizing peppers. There was a mixture of modern spatulas, stainless steel pots and hand-crafted cooking utensils. The further we descended into the lower levels of the market place, the more primitive the goods that were being sold. I was concerned for our safety because I knew we stood out as tourists. I suggested that we look for the exit and end our little adventure in "ethnicity." As we walked towards the exit, a strong fragrance rose from the rows of burlap bags containing exotic spices. I stopped for a moment to inhale this rare olfactory delight. While ascending the stone path leading towards the exit, we saw rows and rows of exquisite yard goods, made from quality bright shiny materials. Mani decided to buy some material to have a couple of dashiki suits made. A little farther up the path was a section of native clothing for children. I was very tempted to buy something cute for Nesya, but I decided to forgo this venture.

Once outside, the sun was so bright that we had to pause for a moment until our eyes adjusted to the light. It was now 2:10 in the afternoon. The photo shop was supposed to re-open at 2:15 p.m. We started walking towards the street on which the photo shop was located. Along the way, Mani again peered in the shop windows which had attracted his attention on the way to the marketplace. By the time we reached the photo shop it was 2:17 p.m. We waited outside the shop, but no one came. We paced back and forth nervously, while looking up and down the intersection for someone who might be hurrying to open the shop, but no one fit that description. The hands on the clock inside the shop approached 2:45 p.m. Still no one came. The midday heat was oppressive, and we were drenched with sweat. My legs ached and my temples throbbed from an intense headache. I knew I had to, at least, find something to drink before I would collapse. Just as we were about to leave to search for something to drink, Mani noticed a man holding keys and walking towards us. None of us could remember if this was the shopkeeper, who had literally closed the door in our faces. We waited to see if he was going to unlock the door. Indeed, he did. We tried to show some restraint and not stampede him when he opened the door. He went inside and situated himself behind the counter. Dora walked over to him and spoke to him in French. I could tell by the way she stiffened her back that what he had said to her was not pleasing. I walked up to her. "He says that he is not the one who takes passport photos and that we will just have to wait." I was dumbfounded. Mani's jaws tightened, and then, he mumbled something under his breath. Well, I thought, at least we have shelter from the searing sun. Since we had no recourse but to wait until the photographer arrived, we chose seats near the bay window in order to observe anyone approaching the shop –as if that was going to make the photographer arrive sooner. I noticed that outside the shop, a street vendor was selling hot coffee from a brass container he was carrying on his back – just the way it was done in Jerusalem in the Old City. This made me a bit homesick, but at the same time, it reminded me of how much I needed to find something to drink. As much as I needed to drink, I still did not have the strength to get up to go and look for a kiosk nearby. Neither did Dora or Mani. So, we just sat and waited for the photographer to come. Because there was not much else to do, I began to notice the peculiar structure of this shop. It was located at the juncture of two major streets. Its entrance was narrow, but the interior widened in the direction of the two adjacent streets. The shop was cone-shaped, with the tip cut off at the point where the doorway was. There was a winged alcove in the eastern wall in the direction of the marketplace. This gave an appearance of a bay window. The upper part of this bay window opened horizontally, and underneath it was a wooden bench built into the wall. An old wooden table stood in front of it. It was sticky from the stains of coffee cups. A rickety ceiling ventilator whirled above it, redistributing the stale air. Suddenly, from outside the window, a shiny round-faced man poked his head through the window and shouted something to the clerk inside. His shout startled Nesya and awakened her from her nap. She looked annoyed but soon became interested in all the commotion near her – a man with a big round face smiling through the window. This man was holding an oval shaped brass tray which hung from brass chains, joined together by a handle. It, too, was quite similar to those used in the Arab section of the Old City of

Jerusalem. On the tray were bottled drinks – fruit drinks and beer. Mani quickly grabbed a bottle of beer and thrust a CI franc bill at him. The bearer threw some CI franc coins back at him. I took out a 50 CI franc note, took two bottles of lemon juice, two bottles of water and a bottle of orange juice from the tray. The man took the bill, and I got no change. As I was opening one of the bottles of lemonade, I noticed the picture on the label. The picture was of an oasis! The drink was not cold, but that did not matter. I gulped it down so fast; it spilled out of the corners of my mouth. Then, I picked up a bottle of water and guzzled it down. Dora filled one of Nesya's bottles with some lemonade and one with some water. The rest she drank. We all looked at the last bottle – the orange juice – like vultures over a prey. I began to giggle inside. I was wondering which one of us would break the code of dignity, pounce upon the bottle and drink it down. We looked at each other again, then at the bottle, and we all began to laugh. It was unanimously agreed upon that we would save it for Nesya.

A few minutes later, another man thrust a tray through the window. Upon it were dishes of rice, greens, and well-seasoned sardines. Other people who had entered the shop quickly bought almost everything on the tray. They pushed and crammed themselves on the benches near us and began to devour their meal. As they ate, they talked and laughed and seemed to enjoy their "outing."

At three o'clock, the two passport photographers arrived. People began to queue-up at the counter to pay their money and get a number which determined who would be photographed first. Not knowing what to expect, we were not the first to get in line. Even so, there were not more than about ten people ahead of us, but the number we were given was 41! How could that be? We sat and waited for our number to be called. Then we noticed that people with higher numbers than ours were being called before us. Both Dora and Mani went to the counter to protest. They were told we would be called shortly. In the meantime, we watched people climb up to the loft where the photos were being taken. This loft was on the western wall near the entrance to the shop. In order to get to it, one had to climb up some rickety stairs made of two-by-four boards nailed together. These make-shift stairs were so narrow that one foot had to be placed in front of the other, while ascending or descending. As I watched people descend, I was a little nervous that they might slip and fall and roll out of the front door. While trying to figure out how I would manage to carry Nesya up these stairs, I noticed someone else with a number higher than ours, climbing up to the loft. I placed myself at the bottom of the stairs and blocked the way of anyone else who might try to ascend before us. After the last person descended, I cautiously climbed up to the loft and sat on the stool in front of the camera. I held Nesya on my lap and prepared her for the photo, while we waited for the photographer to prepare the camera. I was amused at the sight of this camera. It was a square wooden box with an accordion front and a small square frame for the shutter. This camera could have been used to take a picture of Charles de Gaulle when he was a baby. I wondered how pictures taken from this ancient contraption could be accepted by the American Embassy. Nesya was becoming restless from being cooped up in such tiny quarters. I tried to amuse her by drawing her attention to the camera, but she was not at all amused. She refused to smile, and the photographer took her picture any way. Afterwards I tried to descend the narrow steps, but they began to shake underneath my feet. I stood there, frozen like the Statue of Liberty, with Nesya in my arms. Dora had to climb up to meet us, and she took Nesya from me so that I could regain my footing and climb down. I sighed with relief. My legs were still trembling, and I wanted to sit down. The window bench was now occupied by others. There was only one vacant chair, an old chair with a round seat and a back made of two cylinder-shaped pieces of wood, one placed inside the other and twisted to connect to the seat. I sat down on this chair and it swayed back and forth, much like the stairs I had just descended. Dora and Mani stood nearby by. We looked at the clock. It was nearly four o'clock, and the embassy would close at 4:45 p.m. I worried that we would not reach the embassy before it closed. At 4:15, we approached the counter and demanded quicker service. The clerk was offended. Finally, at 4:30 p.m., we received the pictures. The urgency of our mission gave us the strength to run the seven blocks back to the embassy. We arrived at 4:43 p.m. The guards at the barrier had changed. Fortunately, because I had the forms with me, they did not detain me. Inside, the officers recognized me. They scanned my handbag without delay, and I hurried to the room to hand in the forms.

The clerk looked at the pictures and the forms to see if everything was in order. He took them and stamped them and said that it was too late to process them this day and that we would have to return the next morning. The day's ordeal had left me drained of all emotion. I just wanted to get back "home" and lie down. We flagged down a taxi outside the embassy compound and said in unison, "Riveria Place." We were too tired to talk during the ride home, and Nesya fell asleep as soon as we entered the taxi. She snored loudly for the full length of the ride. Besides her snoring, the clicking of the taxi meter and the hum of the motor, we were oblivious to all other sounds and commotions outside.

At some point we all became aware of the slow pace at which we were traveling. When we looked out the front window of the taxi, we noticed that we were behind army jeeps and other armored cars. They were all filled with soldiers. The taxi driver did not try to pass them. I thought that he was probably afraid to do so. Further down the road, we saw groups of soldiers walking along the berm of the road. Their rifles were loaded. Then, for the first time, I noticed that there was a huge military police station which was located about 300 meters from the main road. Why hadn't I noticed this compound before? The convoy turned right and proceeded to the military post. Soldiers were standing in uniformed groups, but in the middle stood someone who must have been their commander because they were giving him their undivided attention. In one group of soldiers, the center of attention was not their officer; it was a map on which he was drawing. Though no one in the taxi spoke, I was sure that everyone was thinking the same thing: "How long would it be before the next military upheaval." Besides the havoc it would play on the local citizens, no one was sure how foreign nationals would be treated, (and all of us staying in the "House" - also known as "The Unofficial Liberian Embassy" – i.e. ULE, were foreign nationals!) I wondered how much I could depend on the U.S. Embassy to come to my rescue if it was necessary.

The residents of "The House" looked at each other in fear and disbelief when we described our day's ordeal. They couldn't understand how such a simple event had become so complicated. After quietly discussing it among themselves, they decided that the seriousness of the situation called for some "hard" praying. I knew what that meant. There would be a gathering that night in "The House" and the group would shatter the heavens with their appeals for divine intervention. What I wanted was some uninterrupted sleep to consume my exhaustion. After going through our evening routine, I placed Nesya in our narrow youth bed and curled up beside her. Immediately after I had said "Shema" (our evening prayer said while reclining in bed), I fell sound asleep. Though I could hear the prayer service in the background, nothing aroused me from the deep sleep with which I was blessed.

The next morning, we went through our morning routine rotely. We climbed into a taxi with a barefoot driver and headed towards downtown Abidjan. We waited in line like good citizens, went through the security checks, and I got a number to enter the office for the processing of my papers. The clerk took my papers and scrutinized them carefully. Then, he called his superiors who also scrutinized them carefully. He carried the papers to another officer, who must have been a superior. She spent a long time looking at each page. Then, she came to the service window, and with a sweet, but serious smile, she said that she could not accept my application for my daughter's passport. She said that we did not meet the U.S. criteria. I tried to clarify what the problem was, but nothing she said made any sense to me. With a firm, "I'm sorry," she pushed my application form and my $32 underneath the window, and called the next applicant to present his forms.

Disbelief gripped me like a vice. Was I an American citizen, or wasn't I? I felt totally alienated and abandoned. Fear and sweat washed over me. I was thousands of miles from **_both_** my homes. I could easily be swallowed up into a country totally foreign to me, and **_no one would be aware of the fact!_** I walked outside holding the application and money in my hand. Dora and Mani looked at each other, trying to comprehend what was going on. I was unable to utter a word.

Finally, I managed to say, "Let's go." Dora and Mani looked at me, waiting for me to explain. I took Nesya in my arms and began to walk away. The two followed. Once we were in the taxi, I told them what had happened. They looked at me in disbelief. I could tell by the looks on their faces that their image of U.S. omnipotence had been sorely damaged.

Once we arrived at "The House," I knew it was of paramount importance to contact people back home in Israel. There were six people whom I considered to be my umbilical cord to the future. Abba Yoske, my kibbutz father. He had immigrated to Israel at a young age and had helped to found a kibbutz in the northern Negev desert. He was practical and rational and very familiar with government policies. The second person was Leah, my Liberian sister, who had started an import-export business in Israel. The third person was Arieh, my immediate supervisor at the school where I taught. He was an immigrant from the former Soviet Union and very familiar with bureaucracy both in Israel and abroad. The fourth person was Ze'ev, the bank manager who handled my bank account. The fifth person was Arienne, a friend of mine from the time we were learning Hebrew on kibbutz. She was very familiar with international law. The sixth person was Vendyl. He was a 70 year-old cowboy who could accomplish things that most people could not. He had been a volunteer in the Six-Day War, and his ability to "think out of the box" greatly contributed to Israel's success in that war. The conversations with all six were pretty much the same:

Me: "Things are getting pretty worrisome here. Another military upheaval is expected any day."

Y/L/A/Z/A/V: "Are you sure? Maybe, you're just so stressed that you're just imagining the worst."

Me: "Yes, I am sure. You can tell from the news reports and from the military movement on the roads."

Y/L/A/Z/A/V: "Maybe, the army is just trying to show their presence in order to keep things under control."

Me: "That could be, but we could see a military police compound with soldiers getting briefings. The compound was not far from the main road on which we travel daily to get to downtown Abidjan."

Y/L/A/Z/A/V: "Now you are exaggerating! How could you see something like that! They wouldn't be carrying out these briefings where everyone could see!"

Me: "Look, I know what I saw! Things are heating up, and soon there is going to be trouble!"

Y/L/A/Z/A/V: "Okay, okay. How can we help you from over here? What do you need? Money? Food?

Me: "I need someone to get me permission to bring Nesya home!"

Y/L/A/Z/A/V: "We'll see what we can do. You know that the Child Welfare Service says you are not qualified to bring her to Israel. They say leave her there; you come back, and they will see what they can do."

Me: "That's ridiculous! I have no intentions to leave her here. I almost lost her once, and I am **_not_** going to go through that again. Please, please, see what you can do. I must get us out of here as quickly as possible."

Y/L/A/Z/A/V: "Look, we will do the best that we can. In the meantime, we will see that you get money to sustain you. Also, get to the Israel Embassy as soon as you can. They might be able to help –despite what Child Welfare Service has decreed. Keep up your spirits."

Me: "When I get back home, I am going to write a book, and I will call it, "Out of Africa."

Y/L/A/Z/A/V: "Sorry, but that book has already been written."

Me: "Well, then I'll call it, "Not Without My Daughter."

Y/L/A/Z/A/V: "Sorry, kiddo, that too has been written."

Me: "Well, then I'll call it, "Out of Africa, but Not Without My Daughter."

Y/L/A/Z/A/V: (chuckles) "Love ya'. Don't worry. HaShem will not desert you."

Me: "Thanks. You're right. I just have to remember that He put me here for a purpose, and He will make a way somehow!"

Chapter Five

WEAR AND TEAR ON MY BODY AND SOUL: VOODOO IN THE MIDNIGHT HOURS

After these phone conversations, the next step was to go to the market place and to the pharmacy. Nesya needed baby supplies, and I had to find something to eat. I felt such wear and tear on my body and soul. Tension and stress were mounting. I was suffering physically, mentally and spiritually. Physically, I was suffering because of lack of food – not that there wasn't an abundance of food in Abidjan. The market places were full of fresh produce. The yams, which I dearly love, stared at me from overflowing bushel baskets. Bananas and plantains as large as elephant tusks and as small as pigmy fingers swung from the overhead frames of vendors' stalls. Tropical fruit of which I had never tasted bade me like the forbidden fruit of Eden to just taste a little. The unrelenting hunger reached out, plucked a juicy mango and dangled it in front of my eyes and whispered to me "Eat, eat you fool. You know what you are missing." But I knew I should not and could not allow myself to eat them. Eating local produce whose sanitary standards were not regulated could, at best, make me sick, and at worst, could kill me. I tried tightening my stomach muscles and told hunger to take a leap into a hot pot of soup. Resisting the odor of freshly baked bread used up the last of my strength. I visualized it as beautiful African genies swirling through the market place, around my head, and then dancing in front of my nostrils. I nearly collapsed right then and there.

"Josefa!" Rachel called out as she caught my arm before I

fell. "Are you all right?!"

"Yes,yes, I . . . just lost my balance for a moment."

"It's probably from hunger," she gently chastised. "Are you sure this bread is not . . . what did you call it 'kosher'? I only buy this woman's bread because I know her house is very clean, and she uses no pork-lard in it."

"Rachel, if I thought that there was any way I could eat it, I would buy every loaf she has here on the stand, and then we would go home and have a feast. I would put it in the middle of the Shabbat table and thank G-d for his goodness and mercy. But "Kosher" is more than cleanliness. It is also self-discipline. I must live up to my part of the bargain if I expect G-d to live up to his."

Rachel, being a strongly religious Christian, could understand being devoted to G-d's will, but she could not fathom why He would expect us to "torture" ourselves for him. I could not expect her to understand, even if I explained in detail the laws of Kashrut (Jewish dietary laws). I could tell, by the look in her eyes, she did not believe that strict observance of Jewish dietary laws was demanded by G-d and that she felt that the Jewish interpretation of G-d's will was just masochism. I respected her and wanted her to understand. It saddened me that though we had shared so much of ourselves in the short time since we had met, we still had no common grounds on which to build understanding and friendship. I realized that the more I would try to explain, the more confusing the issue would become. Sometimes, the less said, the better it is. I decided to end the discussion and turn to another topic – where could I get baby food for Nesya. Though she was a year and a half, her only source of nutrition had been mother's milk and rice porridge. Introducing her to more substantial diet and solid food had to be done gradually. Rachel, whose own adopted daughter, now four years old, had become an expert in infant nutrition and caring for these delicate, malnourished little souls. She suggested that we go to the local pharmacy and buy more baby formulas and commercial vitamin-enriched baby cereals. In addition to the baby formulas, which she was now drinking, we would add baby cereal. At first, we would dilute it to the consistency of milk and later on to the consistency of rice porridge – something like that of buttermilk. This was what Nesya's system was used to. Gradually, we would increase the thickness of the cereal until it was of the consistency of cream of wheat. When she was able to tolerate this consistency, we would introduce cream of wheat into her diet. Then, we would add baby food.   The pharmacy was air-conditioned and immaculately clean. The cool air helped to revive me. While Rachel conversed with the pharmacist, I sat on a window ledge, observing the cordiality and efficiency. When I felt stronger, I stood up and joined Rachel at the counter. There was a heap of baby products piled in front of us. Along with the formula and cereals were diapers and shampoo, and an assortment of skin creams and lotions to heal Nesya's festering mosquito bites. There was a toothbrush and baby bottles and a comb and brush set. Everything was packaged in clear pastel plastic wrapping, with the price printed in the local currency. The money matter had me totally baffled. I could have been paying $20 or $200, for all I knew. The fact is that it really didn't matter. Nesya needed these items. Rachel helped me sort through the colorful monopoly-type money stuffed in my billfold, and I handed the pharmacist a fist full of bills. The total amount was 548 C.I. francs – whatever that meant.

Afterwards, we went to the super market, hoping to find something that I could eat. This was almost a futile ritual, like the previous visits to the super market. We checked all the canned goods. We checked all the dairy products, and we questioned management about the contents of the baked goods. I chose a couple of cans of corn that had been prepared in water and a few yogurts. Next to the dairy section was a clothing section. In a area only about 30 square meters, there was clothing for every age, from babies to adults. I chose a couple of pairs of socks and a cute bib for Nesya. Then, I noticed a toy section. The toys were of high quality. I found a sweet little doll and a squeeze toy for Nesya. For Rachel's daughter who was due to return from Liberia, I found an "etch 'n' sketch" and a numbers book. I was satisfied with my purchases and tried to envision the girls playing with their new toys.

By the time we arrived back at Rachel's, I had little strength left. I sat passively while Dora and Mani prepared the evening meal, fed Nesya, and bathed her. Then, they brought her out to the porch where I was sitting with a few of the residents. Nesya went from person to person, climbing on and off of their laps. They tickled her and teased her, and she giggled. I wanted to extend her moments of happiness and pleasure; so, I gave her the new squeeze toy. Just as she did in the super market, she only looked at it. Then, I gave her the doll. This, too, she only looked at. Suddenly, I realized why she seemed so apathetic. These were the first toys she had ever had, and she didn't know what she was supposed to do with them. I felt true grief at the thought. Never had I met a child who did not know what a toy was. I wanted to cry. I thought about how many children there probably were in the world who had never had a toy. My heart ached for them.

Finally, with a lot of demonstration from all of us, Nesya began to imitate our behavior and play with the toys. At first, she looked a bit puzzled and hesitant. When she first managed to squeeze the rubber dog, the noise it emitted scared her. Then, she tried again and laughed. Afterwards, she demanded that everyone imitate her behavior and squeezed the toy dog. She seemed very proud of herself. The doll was harder for her to relate too. I am not sure if it was the fact that the doll was white or the miniature features of a baby. None of the dolls in the store looked African. None were brown or any other color but white. I thought this was odd considering that we were in an African country. I, then, had a flash-back of my childhood. Brown dolls were hard to find. My father had gone to a lot of trouble to find me a "black" doll. No one knows where he got it, and for many years after he died, none of our friends or families were able to locate a "colored doll."

Not realizing it, we had sat on the veranda until nearly midnight. The weight of fatigue sat heavily on my shoulders; so, I decided I would retire for the night. Mani, Nesya, and I shared a bedroom that was about six by eight meters. The room contained two youth beds with just enough space between them to walk to the window at the far wall. There was a shelf above each bed, and under the shelf was a clothes rack. Mani had a small corner at the end of the bed, and there he stored all his personal belongings. There was a night-stand at the end of my bed, and I used it for Nesya's diapers and bottles. Underneath this night-stand, I placed a cardboard box to store whatever food I had accumulated. Each time either one of us wanted to access our clothing, we had to pull out our suitcases from underneath the bed. Needless to say, modesty could have been a problem, but we had worked out a system to preserve each other's privacy. After changing Nesya's diaper, I put on my nightgown/house coat and climbed into bed bedside Nesya. I looked at the clock, and it was already after midnight. I tried to find a comfortable position, but it was hard with a child who had a tendency to sprawl and twist and turn.

So, I lay in the narrow youth bed, listening to the gentle breathing of my small daughter snuggled next to me. My head was still throbbing from the trials and tribulations of the day. Dora, Mani and I had spent the whole morning and a good part of the afternoon trying to obtain a visa for Nesya. It was arduous at least, and humiliating at best I tried to rest and, maybe, by some miracle, I would fall asleep. My body ached from the cramped sleeping conditions. My head hurt and my mind was weary from the daily ordeal, but I still I could not fall asleep.

At first, it was hardly audible and hardly noticeable – the drum beats in the distance. I strained to listen. Was it just my imagination – my head pounding, or were there really drums beating? After all, we were in the suburbs of a major metropolis. Actually, that was the reason drum beats were audible; we were close enough to the surrounding villages, so their prayers and incantations could be heard. Voices began to accompany the rhythm of the drums. The rhythm was becoming intoxicating and the drum beats began to penetrate my brain. I was certain that those who understood the language were totally hypnotized by the incantations. Both the voices and the drums became louder. Suddenly, a long high shrill pierced the air. It was unsettling. The drums seemed to answer the call of the voice. The tempo was increasing. There were more shrills. Two groups of voices – one leading the calls and one answering, seemed to be trying to overpower the other. Some of the sounds seemed to be angry and some seemed to be mocking. The sounds were beginning to echo off the buildings in Riveria Place. You could hear windows being shut and doors being slammed in the next apartment building. A dog howled in the distance. Crickets in the nearby lagoon chirped with all their might. Were they too disturbed by the cacophony, or were they participating in the ceremony? I heard another animal call, but I could not recognize what it was. I had the feeling that even the dead had been awakened. Maybe, that was the reason for the event. Long, drawn-out banshee screams almost drowned out the drums. When would it end, I asked myself. I looked at the clock in the dimly light hallway. It was now two o'clock in the morning. I felt like screaming, too. Amazingly, no one in Rachel's apartment stirred. The drums and the screams were at such a frantic pace, I could not understand how they could continue much longer – but they did. There was a blood-curdling howl that lasted for what seemed like an eternity, and suddenly, there was silence. I glanced at the clock again. It was now almost three o'clock in the morning. My heart was pounding and my blood was racing like hot lava through my body. This event left me with a sense of fear as if I had seen a horror movie. Even though I was sweating, I pulled the covers up over me to somehow shield from what I had just experienced. I wanted to sleep, but I was afraid. I said, "Shema, Israel" –

" Hear, Oh Israel. The L-rd is G-d, The L-rd is One."

When Rachel came to wake me in the morning, I was too exhausted to move. Every muscle in my body ached. My body had an unusually pungent foul odor, which I could not bear. I wanted to get up and bathe. Yet, I could not seem to move. I hate cold showers, but I felt I needed to stand under cold running water to remove all remnants of the impurities of idolatry. I tried to lift myself up but couldn't. It as if cement blocks were attached to my limbs. Try as I would, I could not sit up. This scared me. Was I becoming ill, G-d forbid?! I knew I could not hold up under my usual daily routine of running from embassy to embassy, trying to get a visa for Nesya and being rejected. I decided that I had to make a change in the day's itinerary. I wanted to immerse myself in whatever Western culture I could find in the area.

"Rachel," I managed to say. "I really feel I must do something different today. Are there any shopping malls in the area?"

"Yes, there is a very nice one called "Soco Cey." Is there anything in particular you want to buy?"

"Well, maybe I'll buy Nesya a doll. Maybe, I'll even find some kosher food."

"It's about time you thought about eating properly. You don't look well. I worry about you."

"I know, but I am so caught up in trying to get home, back to Israel with Nesya, that I can't seem to think about anything else."

"Yes, but your health is also important. How are you going to care for her and get back to Israel if you are sick?"

"I can't argue with that."

"So, today, take a rest from your normal routine, buy some food, relax a bit, and if you feel guilty about "not accomplishing anything," make a few phone calls to some embassies."

"You are a wise woman. I really appreciate your advice."

I lay in bed trying to decide exactly what I would do on my "day off." The phone rang. I could hear Dora speaking in French. I was too tired to try to understand what was being said. My head was void of thought, and I enjoyed it. Then, I heard her call my name. "It's for you – from Israel." I struggled to get up. Leah was on the line. Oh! It was so good to hear her voice. I forced back the tears. She explained to me in brief what the problem was in getting a visa to take Nesya home. It was my age. According to Israeli adoption regulations, a potential adoptive parent must not be more than 45 years older that the child. I was 50 years older than Nesya. Therefore, I would not be granted recognition of the adoption papers issued in Liberia. Anger welled up inside me. How dare they judge me by one factor – one which I had no control over! What gall they had to deny me the right to be a mother. Instead of baring a child out of wedlock, I chose to try to adopt. I remembered the first time I approached the Child Welfare Agency. I was 36 years old. The social worker told me that the cut-off age for adoptive parents was 35; so, I was not eligible. When they decided to raise the age to 40, I was already 42. I was 46 when they raised the age to 45. To whom could I turn to approach the authorities on my behalf? Who could intercede for me? Wasn't there anyway of getting "dispensation" so that I could take my daughter home? Leah said she would try the International Red Cross, but it was located in Geneva. This would surely take time. My money was dwindling rapidly. Leah said she would speak with my bank manager about forwarding me money. Then, she asked about Mani. I told her that he was truly an angel sent from heaven. I called him to come to the phone. Though he had been sleeping, he was on his feet instantly when he heard that Leah was on the phone. They laughed a bit. The sound of laughter was soothing. After Leah hung up, I told Mani that I had decided to change our daily routine and go to the mall, Soco Cey. He sighed with relief. He, too, was exhausted and needed a change. I looked at him and realized that he had a very nice smile. The lines around his mouth softened. His facial muscles relaxed and his eyes sparkled. He looked like an impish boy ready for adventure. He promptly went to tell Dora of our change in plans. I could hear them laughing. Today, would be a day of fun and adventure for all of us. We sat in the hallway on crude wicker foot-stools, planning our new itinerary. The first thing I needed to do was change money to local currency. I could do this in a bank, which would be a drawn-out process with a hefty exchange fee, or I could change money at one of the local street vendors. There were certain "trading points." The trick was to change money and not get ripped off or mugged. Dora suggested trading in Treichville (pronounced "trash-ville"), but Rachel immediately nixed the idea, saying it was too dangerous. There were many change-points in downtown Abidjan, but none of us wanted to see downtown Abidjan today. There was also a supermarket in one of the

100

neighborhoods west of Riveria Place, but Soco Cey was north of Riveria Place. Any way we figured it, we would have to spend a lot of time riding in taxis. We finally decided to go to the supermarket, thinking that maybe I could also fine so kosher food. Since we were already behind schedule, we let the other household members use the bathroom facilities first. I lay back in bed. What a relief not to be hurrying off somewhere. Rachel turned on the radio to BBC Africa. The other house guests crowded around the radio to listen to the news. Rebels in the north of the country were raiding and terrorizing the villagers. Nigeria was experiencing border skirmishes. Sierra Leone was on high alert because of rebels. The guests whispered in French among themselves. Was this because of me? I sensed there was a feeling of concern. I wondered if what was happening in the region was reason for me to be concerned. When I asked Rumia, she avoided my question, and the rest of the guests quickly dispersed. Though I felt uneasy, I was not going to let this ruin my day.

Nesya woke up. She smelled as putrid as I did. I heated water for her bath. There was still hot water in the flask which we used for her night-feedings. I prepared a bottle for her. Then, I realized that that night she had not awakened for a feeding.

It was almost 10 o'clock when we got into the red taxi. We were usually on the road by eight. Since I did not have to concentrate on strategies for dealing with government bureaucracies and embassies, I could sit back and take in the scenery. The Ivory Coast was blessed with such natural beauty. Once out of Riveria Place, we drove along a road which outlined the lagoon. Then it veered away and gently wound through the lush green countryside. We passed by street vendors nestled among the prolific vegetation. Some stalls sold tropical fruit. Others sold drums and handcrafted musical instruments. The most impressive merchandise being sold was the furniture carved from mahogany wood. Some vendors made lawn furniture and some made house furniture. The whole process of furniture-making could be observed along the way. First, there were the piles of tree trunks. Then, there were the pulleys & lifts for moving the tree trunks to the cutting area. There were no massive saw mills – just simple cutting machinery. On the right were the tree trunks and to the left were the piles of lumber. Some pieces of lumber were neatly cut and others seemed to be hand –chiseled. Since we were moving rather quickly in the rickety old taxi, I tried to observe at least a different stage of furniture-making at each vendor. The next stage seemed to be laying the pieces to be assembled in close proximity to each other. Then I could see chaise-lounge chairs being constructed. The ingenuity of the craftsmen was simply amazing. The utility of each chair and table had to have been foremost in its creator's mind. Drawers and serving trays could be pulled out for use, and when tucked away, becoming an invisible part of the decorative design. The wood was finished with a natural wood stain, almost the color of the people. Some was varnished to mirror-like brilliancy. Some had lattice-worked backs in which hand-stuffed colorful cushions were placed.

Further down the road, I noticed an unusually beautiful canopy double bed. The intricate design was breathtaking. Oh, how I wanted to buy that bed and take it home to Israel. I rolled down the window of the taxi to get a better look and strained to gaze at it until it was out of sight. Then, I looked for other such beds. There were other simpler versions, but nothing as astounding as that one. I tried to picture myself lying in it in my bedroom in Kiryat Arba, inhaling the fragrance of the wood. Oh, what serenity that could bring!

By now, we had left the village furniture market and were approaching a major highway intersection. It looked like Midwest USA, except that the large iridescent green signs were in French. I noticed one of the blue and grey busses stopped at the traffic light. The people crammed inside were sweating profusely. I was glad that we could afford the "luxury" of a taxi. The fact was that no busses served the inner streets of Riveria Place.

A knock on the window of the taxi startled me. Then, I realized that the taxi was surrounded by young boys and men holding up objects which they wanted to sell. Some had simple objects such as facial tissue or nail clippers, but others had electric shavers and radios or boom boxes. Others carried an assortment of newspapers. The young men were persistent, and I became frightened. As soon as the light changed, the driver floored the gas pedal and we sped away. I looked back at the men, holding up their wares, running and screaming after us. We were soon on a major highway, heading towards the supermarket, where I could change money and maybe find some kosher canned goods. I looked at the taxi- meter. The numbers were changing at a furious pace. I wondered if I had enough local currency to pay for this trip. I didn't want the driver to know we were going to change money. When you're in a foreign country, you can never be too careful. When we finally pulled into the parking lot in front of the supermarket, we had to pool our money in order to pay the driver. I'll bet he was wondering what we were going to buy food with.

The "supermarket" was a miniature of what I had expected. It was just a local grocery store with two checkout counters and crowded aisles. I looked for the canned good section while Dora bartered with the shop owner for the dollar rate. Mani wandered down each aisle, looking for the kosher symbols I had described to him. He came running to me with a can of Spam and showed me the Registered symbol, which he mistook for the "OU" found on kosher products. The shelves of canned goods were plentiful, but not one single product had an "OU", nor even a "K" for that matter. In order for the shopkeeper to change our money, we had to buy something. I picked up a package for facial tissue and looked around for something else I could buy. Seeing the "350 C. I. Francs" on a bottle of fruit juice scared me. I looked for something cheaper. Then, I noticed the shelves filled with an assortment of potato chips and corn chips. I rummaged through them all, and then I stared in disbelief at a large bag of potato chips which had an "OU." I startled the shop owner and Dora when I shouted, "I found it! I found it!" You would have thought that I had discovered gold. I grabbed three bags and ran to the counter. Two bags were left on the shelf, and I debated whether to buy them to.

At the counter, Dora told me what the exchange rate was. I asked her if it was good. She said that it wasn't the best, but since none of us had any money left, we had better take it. I handed him two $50 travelers' checks and received 291.600 C.I. Francs in return. This really seemed like Monopoly money. With this, I paid for the chips and tissue and we headed out to flag down another taxi to take us to Soco Cey. Again, we were on a major highway, but the scenery did not seem like Midwest USA. It seemed like southern California, with palm trees lining the many boulevards. "There it is!" Dora said. "That's Soco Cey!" I was astonished. The mall was a massive complex. Huge colorful flashing signs, bearing the names of the movie theater, fashionable clothing shops, and a supermarket, were attached to the side of the building. Once inside, one could forget in which country he was. The only thing that reminded people that they were, indeed, in Africa were the stands displaying African figurines in the entrance. It was as if they were purposely placed there to say, "You are in Africa, in Abidjan, the Paris of Africa." I surmised that they had been placed there to help orient people suffering from a sudden attack of cultural shock. I looked at the waterfall and the glass elevators, descending and ascending, thinking that western culture can be found within a twenty-minute ride from an African village. Besides the African figurines at the entrance, the only thing that hinted that we were in Africa was the colorful dresses and flowing dashikis that the people were wearing. Mani was a maven for western culture. The first thing he noticed was the Internet cafe and a sign advertising foreign calling cards. He went to check it out while I held Nesya and discussed with Dora what I was hoping to buy. The Internet cafe was so crowded that we decided to leave that for last.

We found a floor plan of the mall and looked at the names of the shops. Everything was upscale. We decided that before we started our search for kosher food in the supermarket, we would go up to the top floor, walk around and work our way down to the supermarket on the first floor. It was good to know that there was a Western Union office there. There was also a very nice baby boutique and a toy store. I thought that at some point, I would buy a few items for Nesya and a toy for Rachel's daughter. Mani looked at the men's clothing stores and at the watches next to the diamonds in the jewelry store. Dora seemed aloof and not very interested in window- shopping. Nesya was beginning to fidget; so, we quickened our pace.

The supermarket was well-planned, well-stocked, and well-laid out to entice people to buy. Children's school supplies, books and magazines were to the right of the entrance. To the left, were toys on sale and children's beach wear. Behind the books and magazines were the aisles with small electrical appliances. On the opposite side of the aisle were dishes and kitchen appliances. But, the most "tasteful" part of the layout was the bakery at the far end of the store, directly opposite the entrance. The smell of the freshly baked baguettes was overwhelming. Well, smells are free, and I inhaled deeply the fragrance of this enormous temptation. I looked at the line of people and thought that the bread must surely be good. Being a little bit masochistic and a little bit hopeful, I checked the ingredients on the shelved bread. There was pumpernickel, rye, oat, French, and Italian bread. Though the labels said "vegetable oil", I knew that there could be a problem. Baguettes usually are "kosher", but because there was cheese bread being sold alongside of them, I could not be sure if they were baked on the same racks as the cheese bread, which was certainly not kosher.

On the way to the canned goods aisles, I picked up two blue plastic plates, two forks, two teaspoons, two tablespoons and two paring knives. Then, I found two interesting plastic cups and a medium- sized aluminum pot. I was sure I would find something I could prepare to eat.

And I did! Sardines, yogurts, butter, crackers, and peanut butter – all with the OU kosher symbol. None of the canned vegetables had an OU or a "star k", or a "triangle K." I was disappointed. I began scrutinizing the labels. I chose some cans of corn and peas and green beans, which were cooked only with salt and water.

Then we headed for the fresh fruits and vegetables. I chose apples and bananas, kiwis, and peaches. I figured that this store must hold by some sanitary regulations. Potatoes and carrots or anything grown in the ground, I decided to forgo.

Our fingers became numb from rummaging through the frozen food cases. Dora pointed out that the refrigerator in the apartment was very small and not working properly; so, even if I found something kosher, there was no way to store it.

The most bulky items on our list were disposable diapers and bottled water. There were long aisles of name brand disposable diapers and bibs, and other baby necessities were tucked in here and there on the shelves or stacked on portable racks in the aisle ways. This enticed you to look at other baby products. Mani seemed to enjoy browsing through the baby supply section. He squeezed rubber toys, compared baby bottle nipples, and sniffed baby powder. He was the one who made the final decision on what we bought for Nesya.

Nesya, too, was enjoying our outing. Her eyes were wide with wonder and amazement. She pointed at items which particularly attracted her attention. She reached for items on the shelves. She even managed to grab hold of a little doll which she liked. With one hand she clutched him to herself, and with the other, she held a can of apple sauce. This, she abandoned when she saw a jar of peanut butter with a bright red lid. She sang out loud her two-syllable baby words. People smiled at her, and she responded with a big grin, showing her four front teeth with the gaps beside them, where the canine teeth would eventually grow-in. The clerks who were stacking the shelves would come over and tickle her. She would giggle and sway back and forth in the cart-seat and sing even louder. Customers walking up and down the aisle smiled. Children whispered to their parents and pointed at her. Nesya extended her little index finger and motioned for them to come over to her, which they promptly did. As they held on to her finger, she gibbered and sang to them. Their wide smiles indicated how much they enjoyed being with her. When their parents called them, they found it hard to leave her. They looked back over their shoulder as she waved to them. It was like this on all our subsequent trips to Soco Cey.

Our last stop before getting in the check-out line was the bottled water section. We got a large supply, and on the way to the cashier, we even found 100% pure apple juice. The total cost was 23,158 C.I. Francs. I laughed. *__I could now be considered "a big spender."__*

We pushed our full carts to the entrance of the mall. We stopped for a moment in front of the Internet cafe, while Mani went inside to check out the rates of long distance calls. Calling long distance from Rachel's flat was almost impossible. The times that we tried to, someone came on the line and the line went dead. I was certain that all overseas phone calls from private homes were being intercepted by the government. Mani returned with a phone card and a list of internet rates. We queued up in the taxi line. It was handled very efficiently. Young men, in burgundy gold-button jackets, pushed our carts to a taxi which had stopped in front of us. He carefully placed our bags in the trunk, bid us a "Good Day", and signaled for the next taxi to pull up to the loading point. I was impressed. I settled back in the back seat and both Nesya and I fell asleep. It had been a fruitful, productive day.

When we arrived at Rachel's house, Dora took Nesya to our bedroom and tucked her in. Mani helped me sort out the groceries on the oval dining room table. Then, I went to check the telephone messages, which were waiting for me in the hallway: one from Leah, one from Air France, one from Sara, and one from the Israel Embassy in Abidjan. Leah: "I have contacted the International Red Cross, and they want me to send them more information." Air France: "All stand-by reservations are full for the next three weeks." Sara: "We are trying to speak with the head of Child Welfare." The Israel Embassy: "Please, contact us as soon as possible." I looked at the wall clock hanging above the telephone. The Embassy office was closed for the day. I already knew what the next day's agenda would entail. Mani passed by me, carrying the packages of disposable diapers which were to be stored against the wall of our crowded bedroom. He returned with the canned goods I had purchased and placed them in the box on the floor between the wall and the foot of the bed. While he was working, I told him about Leah's call and about the phone message from the Embassy. "Well," he said, "I guess I know what our agenda is for tomorrow – downtown Abidjan." We both sighed heavily.

This thought we put behind us and planned our evening activity. First of all, we were going to eat! Then, I noticed the smell of fried fish, greens and rice, floating in from the kitchen. It had been Rumia's turn to prepare the communal meal, and from the "smell of things", she had done a very good job. Dora was in the kitchen grinding hot peppers in a hollowed-out tree stump and a roughly hewn pestle. Three other guests were sitting on foot- stools along the inner wall of the kitchen, piles of dried fish at their feet. They were de-boning them for tomorrow's spicy fish sauce. They bantered in English, French, and Pele, their tribal tongue. Then, they began to sing church hymns as they worked. None of the words were familiar to me but the melodies reminded me of spirituals which I had sung as a child. They harmonized beautifully. One of them began to beat a spoon of the rim of a pot. The two others began to clap out rhythms. Rumia and Rachel began to dance, the way people do when they "get happy" in church – hands raised above their heads as they swayed to the rhythm of the music. One of the three guests took over the solo part. The rest of the group echoed her and sang, "Amen." When they had finished singing, they praised each other with "Amen, sister." By then, the food was ready and each carried a dish to the dining room table. The table had been set with a lovely red lace table cloth, plates made of pottery and red linen napkins placed in each glass. Everyone sat down at the table, and Rachel said "grace." It included thanks for the food they were about to eat, thanks for surviving another day, and blessings for each of those seated at the table. When she had finished, everyone said, "Amen." And, thus, was the morning and the evening of the fifteenth day.

Chapter Six

TREATMENT IN TREICHVILLE

(pronounced "Trash –ville")

The next morning I called the Israel Embassy to make an appointment to meet with the ambassador. The appointment would be the next day. So, we decided to use our time wisely and return to Dr. Quanton at the Cocodey clinic for Nesya to have a progress check-up. Rachel suggested that later on, we visit her at the International School where she worked. I was looking forward to this because I had heard that children from the Israeli Embassy attended school there, and in the center of the campus was a flag for each of the foreign countries. I wanted to see the Israeli flag. I wanted a chance to speak Hebrew and to feel a touch of home.

Dr. Quanton was quite warm and gentle at our next meeting. She was pleased with Nesya's progress, but she was still concerned that Nesya should not have any other health complications. She formulated a nutrition plan and an inoculation program. Since health concerns were different in each country, Nesya would have to start an inoculation program which should have been started when she was three months old. The nearest clinic was in Treichville, nearly an hour's drive from Riveria Place. Dora did not look so pleased at the thought of going there. As we approached Treichville, I could *smell* why Treichville was objectional. The whole area smelled of sewage and rotten meat. The odor was so stifling, it was almost unbearable. Once inside the town, I had the feeling that I had been transported through a time tunnel, back 75 years to a slum community in the United States. There was loud hip-hop music blasting at every street corner. The sidewalk pavement was covered with flattened old wads of chewing gum and globs of phlegm. The hot summer breeze blew swirls of discarded newspapers, cigarette butts, and candy wrappers around our ankles. The shop windows boasted female mannequins wearing sheer red, gaudy royal blue, cheap purple, and revealing black and white dresses. An over-abundance of embossed gold necklaces and bracelets adorned the apparel. The male mannequins wore dashing white suits and Gatsby hats. They gazed sensually towards the female mannequins positioned below them, beckoning them to accompany them to some sleazy nightclub. Every third store graced its windows with fine, highly polished leather shoes. Squeezed in between the clothing and shoe stores were "rib joints." All the store- fronts were old and run-down. They had all shifted from their original structural position and were leaning either to the right or to the left. The imitation tile roofing, which had once been red or green, was now a dull brown with tiny shiny flecks of gold glimmering beneath the years of build-up of grime. The white paint around the door frames was dirty and peeling.

As we walked down a few blocks of the main street, the men who sat on the stoops outside the storefronts looked at us curiously. Flashy pimps standing on two sides of the corners of the intersection scrutinized us. Crude, ostentatious drug dealers glanced over their shoulders at us as we passed by. I hoped we were not attracting too much attention. It was well-known that in Treichville, muggings took place in broad daylight. We were "foreigners" and could be easy prey.

Finally, we reached the side street on which the clinic was located. This street flowed with slime. On each side were vendors selling live chickens, spices, and kitchenware. After about a twenty-minute walk, we arrived at the clinic at the lower end of the street. The outside looked like a run-down cowshed. There was a long line of people waiting to get into the clinic. Most of the women were dressed in traditional African dress. Their flowing gowns were made of bright flowered or print cotton cloth. They wore contrasting head-wraps. They carried their babies and young children on their backs, in a long piece of cloth, which was wrapped around their waist and then tied in front above one of their breasts. I was amazed that I never saw this cloth dirtied by pee-pee stains or "pooh." Later on, I was told that there was a natural instinct for the baby to only "make" when he was removed from this pouch. Another thing that amazed me was how young some of the mothers seemed to be. Some seemed to be no older than 13 or 14 years old. The clinic was not "women's only" territory. Many young men had accompanied their wives. The fathers seemed very proud of their off-springs. They showed a lot of what is termed "maternal instincts."

When we were finally able to get inside the clinic, a nurse took our documents to process them, and we were directed to sit on one of the many long roughly-hewn wooden benches. The clinic ante-room might have been primitive, but the treatment rooms were immaculate - and so was the staff, which spoke several local dialects, as well as French. One concern of mine was the re-use of needles. My fears were assuaged when I saw the "contamination" container with the large bright-red warning sticker with a picture of a syringe and needle.

The nurses were gentle and caring and **_very_** efficient. They explained what injections were being given and why. I was pleased to know that even the "natives" were being given proper medical care. Nesya was so used to getting injections twice a day, one more injection did not faze her. She just stared with disinterest at the needle as it pricked her arm. After the necessary papers had been stamped and signed, we made our way through the waiting room, which was now filled with a new group of people. While we had been waiting, I counted nearly 200 people in the waiting room. Now there were nearly 200 more. To my calculations, if only a third of those present were children waiting to receive inoculation, more than 100 children were being treated daily. That was quite a workload!

After leaving the clinic, we carefully began to ascend the slime-covered street. Once we reached the top of the street, we noticed that a different set of young pimps had taken their position at the corners. This group did not seem to notice us. They were busy making transactions. We walked a block or two along the litter-strewn street until we found a taxi stand. In front of the taxi stand was a little kiosk. There, we bought "drinks for the road" before we got into the taxi. Nesya immediately fell asleep, and we stared out the windows at the infamous city, "Treichville." A few miles outside the city, we breathed a breath of fresh air, as we left the stench behind us.

Mani suggested that, maybe, we should go to the

International School to see Rachel. I liked this idea very much. Dora asked the taxi driver to stop near a pay phone along the way so that we could get directions. Pay phones were not that easy to find, but taxi drivers are very astute about things like this. In minutes, he found one near a major thoroughfare. Dora got instructions from Rachel, and we started off on our next adventure of the day.

When the driver stopped in front of the school, I thought he had made a mistake. There was a simple wire fence around a partially paved parking lot. We got out of the taxi and began to walk to the far end of the parking lot. As we got closer to the other end, I noticed a simple sign that said, "International Facility for Education." Several Guards checked our passports and then questioned us why we had come. We told them that we had come to see Rachel. They seemed to know who she was. A guard picked up an internal phone and asked to speak to Rachel. Another guard opened the gate and told us to wait inside. Soon, Rachel appeared. She looked so official and important, but she gave us all a hug. Then, she took us along one of the side paths to show us the beautiful gardens and waterfalls between the buildings within the campus. It looked much like a kibbutz, with lush vegetation framing each building. Along the way, she met fellow workers who seemed to respect her highly. Finally, she led us to the central courtyard where the national flags of all the countries which were represented at the school could be viewed. Among thirty or more flags, the only flag I noticed was the Israeli flag. I stood like Lot's wife. I could not move. An avalanche of tears rose up in my eyes and flowed down my cheeks and splashed on my clothes. I am not sure how long I cried. I was aware of nothing and no one around me. My heart ached as if I had been hit squarely in my chest. I wanted to approach the flag and hug it and tell it all my sorrows. I wanted to tell it how much I wanted to go home, how much I missed Israel, how much I missed the Western Wall, how much I missed the Tomb of the Patriarchs in Hebron, where Sara and Avraham, our parents are buried.

By the time I stopped crying and regained my composure, I was so weak I could hardly stand. Rachel offered to take us to her office so that she could give me something to drink, but first I wanted to have my picture taken, standing beside the Israeli flag. Afterwards, I felt much calmer and was even able to laugh and joke.

Rachel's office was really a foyer to other offices. Then, I discovered why. The interior offices were stocked with food rations, bottled water, and war supplies, in case there was another coup d'etat. This brought me back to the reality of the situation I was in. I tried not to ask too many prying questions, but what I had learned was that during the previous "coup" the staff and children were caught on campus and had to wait to be evacuated. For an adult, this would have been very traumatic. I wondered how the children had coped with this horrifying ordeal. My thoughts began to race in every direction. How would I cope in such a situation? Where would I be when the "coup" started. How safe was Rachel's apartment, considering the number of foreign nationals who were staying there.

"Josefa?!" I heard my name called. It was Rachel trying to get my attention. "I had wanted to introduce you to some of the Israeli children and teachers, but it is late in the day, and almost everyone has gone home. Maybe, I can bring you here another day."

"That will be fine. Anyway, I think it's time we went home. I am sure you are also tired."

We said "Good-bye" to the guards, walked out to the main road, and flagged down a taxi. On the way home, we passed the military compound and watched the sunset over Abidjan.

Chapter Seven

Elan Vital Embassies:

The Israel Embassy and The Liberian Embassy

For the first time in a long time, I was happy to be getting into a taxi to go to downtown Abidjan. I felt excitement knowing that I was going to the Israel Embassy. A part from the Israeli flag, this façade was the closest place to being home in Israel. The taxi stopped outside the parking lot of an office complex near the embassy. There were no signs that any important office was present in the area. We tried to ask passersby about the location of the embassy, but each one just shrugged his shoulders and kept walking. After several wrong turns in the building complex, we finally found an entrance where a uniformed military person stood. I was not sure what his affiliation was because the insignias were bewildering. However, when I asked, "Can you tell me where the Israel Embassy is?" he pointed to the stairwell and said, ". . . two floors up." When we reached the second floor, there was an iron gate which prevented us from entering. Two guards stood opposite the gate. I told them that the ambassador had summoned me. They asked me to show them some form of identification. I handed them my Israeli passport. They looked at the passport, looked at me, looked through the passport again, and then they pressed the buzzer which unlocked the gate. Mani and Dora followed me into the small foyer. The guards then looked at Mani, Dora, and Nesya and asked me who they were. I told them that Nesya was my adopted daughter for whom I wanted a visa to take her back to Israel and that

Mani and Dora were helping me during my stay in Abidjan. The guards pointed to a conveyor belt, which was connected to a security scanner. I put my hand-bag on the scanner and walked through the metal detector scanner. One of the guards told me to take the elevator up one more floor, but Mani, Dora, and Nesya had to wait in the foyer. We looked at each other with disappointment clearly apparent in our eyes. They sat down to wait for me and I went up in the elevator to the next floor. When I arrived at the next floor, the procedure was a repeat of what I had just experienced. The elevator door opened and immediately in front of it was another iron gate with two guards standing opposite it. I told them what my purpose was for coming. They checked my passport, released the iron gate, and pointed to the security scanner. On the other side of the metal detector scanner were two more guards. Only after they received a signal from the guards at the gate did they press the buzzer to open the internal doors which led to another waiting room. There were several people of all different nationalities sitting on the benches. Each person was holding some kind of official looking form. I approached the reception desk to state my purpose. The receptionist checked the appointment list and told me that I would probably have to wait about twenty minutes. This surprised me because at the other embassies the estimated waiting period was much longer. So, I sat and waited with the rest of the people sitting on the benches. I learned later that not everyone in the waiting room was there to see the ambassador. Only those with the most complicated issues were having a meeting with him, and I was next in line to see him. Twenty-two minutes later, I was called into an inner office where an assistant reviewed my documents. Then, she took them into the ambassador.

Shortly afterwards, she came out and sat down on one of the two chairs facing me. A minute or two later, a medium-height, slightly bald man appeared, carrying my documents. The first thought which came to my mind was that this was a special occasion. One rarely has the opportunity or privilege to meet a dignitary of this sort. My second thought was what had been the chain of events that led to him filling such a position in such a strange country. I wondered if he enjoyed his work. I wondered about his family and how they managed to survive in Abidjan. I had only been there for three and a half weeks, and I could not wait to get on the plane and return to Israel. My thoughts were interrupted when he greeted me in Hebrew. This was like having a soothing balm gently dabbed on my face. I had to wait a moment before I could reply. Hearing Hebrew spoken had put me in a state of euphonic euphoria. When he asked me if I preferred that he speak to me in English, I snapped out of the trance and responded that I preferred to speak in Hebrew. He asked me to explain to him how I had gotten to Abidjan and what my goals were for the future. I summarized the last three years of my life in about twenty sentences. He re-read my documents and handed me three additional forms to fill-out. Then, the words I had most regretted hearing were stated in an empathetic tone, "There is very little chance that a visa will be granted for your daughter. I have reviewed the rules and regulations of the Department of Interior and the Child Welfare Agency. The Department of Interior will only grant a visa if the CWA agrees to it. And as you probably know, the CWA is very strict about 'sticking to the rules'." My mind went blank. I could not think of anything to say. Then, he added, "However, I will contact both authorities and see what I can do. Be in touch with me in a couple of days. In the meantime, fill-out these forms and leave them at the front desk. When you call, ask for my secretary and leave your name. She will tell you what the next step is."

After thanking him for his consideration and help, I went out to the waiting room to fill-out the forms. At first, I could only sit and think about what he had said. I had absolutely no idea what the outcome would be of my trying to take Nesya back to Israel. I wondered how much longer I would be in Abidjan. I felt anger and hatred well-up inside me, though I was not sure towards whom or what these feelings were directed. Then, I realized I was humming an old Negro Spiritual, "Where shall I go? Where shall I go? Where shall I go but to the L-rd?" This song reminded me of my obligation to turn to HaShem and to always keep Him in the picture. I knew He was observing me and what was happening to me, and I was certain that HaShem was in control of the situation. I just had to keep the channels of communication open with Him so that He could guide me. With this thought in mind, I gave the forms to the secretary and went out to meet Mani and Dora. Nesya stretched out her arms for me to pick her up. I hugged her tightly. It felt so good to be with her. As we left the building I explained to Mani and Dora what the situation was. All we could do now is wait for a call from the ambassador's secretary. There was a peculiar feeling in the air during the ride back to Riveria Place. I could not exactly put my finger on what the strangeness was, but it made me feel uneasy. I tried to concentrate on the rode and the surrounding scenery. I looked at the mobs of people congregating on the streets. I wondered why they were milling around, what they were talking about. My attention was drawn to gigantic banners at the corners of each intersection. In huge letters, the signs shouted, "This year, let's stamp out polio!" It was obvious from their ragged, dusty appearance that these signs had been there for some time. I wondered why I had not noticed them before. I guess I was just too wrapped up in my own affairs to notice that the citizens of the Ivory Coast had their own issues and problems. As we rode along the main boulevard to Riveria Place, I saw a tragic sight which made me gasp. There were several young people whose bodies were so deformed that they looked like they had been mangled in the back of a garbage truck. One young man was being carried on the back of another young man. There was no way he could maneuver by himself. Then, I noticed a young boy, probably about thirteen or fourteen years old. His body was so contorted that he could only move about by thrusting himself forward on blocks of wood, which were attached to his forearms. Then, I understood the importance of those huge banners. These poor souls had survived a severe, debilitating bout of polio! How could it be that in the twenty-first century people were still victims of this horrible disease, and it was evident that, somehow, the countries in this area had been overlooked in the war against polio?

The images of these polio victims stayed in my mind for the rest of the evening. I was trying to understand why African nations were crippled, both economically and physically. For many years, they had been controlled by European colonization. What had happened to these nations during this time? The Europeans had certainly benefitted from the natural resources of the land, but what had they given to the countries? What had the local people gained from the colonization? After we prepared for bed - Mani in his narrow bed and snoring quietly, and Nesya curled up beside me in our youth bed – I began to reflect on the history of mankind. I started with Noach (this is the Hebrew pronunciation of Noah in the Bible).

The name Noach, in Hebrew, means "rest" or "comfort." It is very appropriate for a man to want to rest, after having spent such a long time confined in a boat with lots of smelly animals. He probably had to work very hard, and after the flood had receded and he could leave the boat, all he wanted to do was to **rest**! It's no wonder that the first thing he did was to plant a vineyard, make some wine, as soon as the grapes were ripe, and to drink a big cup of it. Well, Noach had three sons, who probably had not yet indulged in the pleasure of the "fruit of the vine." They were probably sitting around, chatting and writing their memoirs for future generations. Shem was Noach's oldest son. Shem, in Hebrew, means "name." "Ham" (pronounced "Hahm") means "warm" or "hot." Yafet means "to stretch out, to extend forward. It is believed that names affect the name-bearers, and we can see the traits or characteristics in the three sons' descendants. From biblical sources, we know in which part of the world the descendants settled.

Shem settled in the Middle-East, staying close to the area which gave the world monotheism. His descendants preserved the Name (i.e. the name of G-d). There were no additions or substitutes for G-d's name.

Ham's descendants settled mainly in Africa. (Notice the connection between the meaning of the name Ham and where his descendants settled.) Ham had four sons: Cush,

Mizraim, Fute, and Canaan. The most well-known sons of Cush were: Raamah and Nimrod. Raaman was the father of Sheba. Nimrod was a hunter, and he was instigator of the building of the Tower of Babel. The root meaning of his name is "rebellion." Egypt is still known, even today, by its ancient name, "Mizraim," in Hebrew, and in Arabic "Mizra." Mizraim was the father of two tribes – Pathrusim and Casluhim, which merged to become the tribe "Philistines." The most famous Philistine was Goliath. The meaning of Philistine is "those who invade." After World War I, when Britain became the protectorate of what is now the State of Israel, they chose to call the area "Palestine," which is a modern form of the name Philistine. The name the British chose is also indicative of their task in the Middle-East.

The name "Fute" seems to have lost any connection with recent history, but the name "Canaan" has been referenced to for many centuries. Some of Canaan's descendants settled in Sidon (Lebanon), while others went further south.

Yafet's descendants settled in what is now Europe and the Far-East. They were seafarers, who extended their influence and culture wherever they traveled. Magog is associated with . . . . . (Russia?). Madai is associated with Persia. Yavan is today's Greece (and is still referred to as such in modern Hebrew). Ashkenaz is Germany. Today's European Jews are called "Ashkenazim."

So, what's in a name? Greece was one of the most influential nations in ancient times. It spread its influence and culture far beyond its "natural" borders. The Romans "inherited" this "gift" of influence. Both of these great powers over-extended themselves, until they could no longer enforce their rule in their colonies. This over-extension was accompanied by a strong sense of arrogance and elitism. The indigenous people of their colonies were not always willing to accept the culture that was imposed upon them. The dissention and lack of rule from a central authority was finally the demise of these great powers.

More recent examples of the arrogance and expansion of Yafet's descendants are Mao Tsutung in China, the War in Viet Nam, the conglomerate of the USSR, Japan's bombing of Pearl Harbor, and, of course, Germany, Hitler, and the vast cruel destruction in Europe in World War II.

Ham, which at one end of the scale, means "warm," at the other end means "hot." Historically speaking, Ham's descendants traveled as far as the Black Sea in Europe. Their intentions did not seem to be to conquer, but rather to extend their trade routes of gold and exotic produce. Some have seen this lack of zealousness to promote African culture as evidence that Africans were culturally limited. This is (and was) far from the truth, considering that the first library of the ancient world was established in Timbuktu, Mali. Ham's descendants were true to their name. They were a warm people, very family oriented and very proud of their tribal affiliation. This often led to internal tribal warfare. Slavery was the result of tribal warfare and European expansionism. The combination of these two elements led to the colonization of Africa and unlimited exploitation of the continent's wealth and natural resources.

Europeans have used the story of Ham in the book of Genesis to justify their involvement in the slave trade. They even used this biblical passage to legitimize perpetuating one of the cruelest acts against humanity:

Genesis 9:18 -25

"And the sons of Noach that went out of the ark were Shem and Ham and Yafet; and Ham is the father of Canaan. These are the three sons of Noach: and from them the whole earth was populated. Noach had been a farmer, and he began to plant a vineyard. He drank from the wine and got drunk, and thus, lay naked in his tent. Ham, the father of Canaan, saw his father naked and told his two brothers. Shem and Yafet took an outer garment, put it upon their shoulders and went in backwards to cover the nakedness of their father. Noach awoke from his wine and knew what his younger son had done to him. He said, "Cursed be Canaan – a servant of servants he will be to his brethren."

There is *one* detail that supporters of slavery overlooked. It was Canaan, Ham's youngest son who was cursed. Ham, himself, was not cursed, and neither were his other sons. In addition to this, Canaan did not settle in Africa; he and his descendants settled in Lebanon and in parts of the Sinai peninsula.

So, why did there seem to be a curse on the Africa continent? With all its wealth and resources, prosperity was far from the grasp of most Africans. This thought troubled me and did not allow me to rest. Why? Why? Why have Africans been looked down upon, and why are the majority of the people still living in poverty? Why have outsiders been able to take advantage of Africans? I had more questions than I had answers. As I tried to relax my mind, a piercing thought penetrated my brain. It shocked me and frightened me. As a child growing up in a less than affluent African-American community, I remembered the stereotypes of Africans portrayed on television. I remembered Tarzan and what Africans were supposed to be like – naked and stupid. I remembered how I, too, had laughed at Africans. I also remembered how we, as African-Americans (then called "coloreds" and "Negroes"), made fun of each other. We played "the dozen." We would make fun of each other until the derogatory remarks ended in tears or a fist-fight. I remembered the bantering of insults on the school bus, when we were being bussed to school. I always prayed that the taunters would not notice me. I had not developed the skills to banter back in rap rhythm and speed. I usually tried to pretend I was sleep or totally engrossed in some thought while staring out the window. Most of the time, I managed to escape the verbal cruelty, but not always. When they did start teasing me, it was because I enjoyed learning, and that was not considered "cool." By the time we arrived at school, I was totally exhausted. My legs were weak, and I could hardly concentrate in my first classes. I "succeeded" in failing a couple of subjects because of this atmosphere of self-contempt. This self-belittlement, this poking fun at ourselves, had a colossal effect on our ability to pull ourselves up by our "bootstraps." We did not allow ourselves to take advantage of the talents that G-d had given us. We were carrying inside of us a form of Lupus disease, where we turned upon ourselves to "self-destruct." ***This is exactly what Ham had done when he made fun of his father!*** This terrifying thought stayed with me until I was finally able to fall asleep.

The next morning I was awakened by Rachel, telling me that someone from the Israel Embassy wanted to speak with me. It was the secretary, saying that the ambassador wanted to meet with me in two days, but first I had to go to the Liberian Embassy to have Nesya's adoption papers reviewed, signed, and stamped "legal" by the Liberian Embassy. This made me jump to my feet, because I knew that I had to get to the Liberian Embassy as soon as possible. There was already a line of people in Rachel's kitchen, either trying to cook breakfast or trying to heat water. I could not wait for them to free-up the kitchen. I was going to have to bathe in **cold water.** For me, this was equivalent to torture. I shivered and shook the whole time I was in the bathe. When I poured the chilly water down my back, I almost screamed, but my thoughts were too much ahead of the cold water splashing over my body. Dora and Mani could have been soldiers the way they jumped to the occasion and were ready to go within minutes. They even had Nesya dressed, fed, and ready for our journey.

We quickly flagged down a taxi and headed for the Liberian Embassy, which was located in a less posh part of downtown Abidjan. If I hadn't known better, I would have thought that I was in one of Brooklyn's ghettos. The embassy was located in a building that looked like a rundown brownstone tenement. The sidewalks were broken and uneven. People sat around on stoops. They were shiny from sweat and had des-interested looks on their faces. The walls in the hallway were covered with graffiti, and the paint was peeling from the ceiling, leaving white powdery dust everywhere, including on those who entered and exited the building. Both Dora and Mani looked embarrassed because of the shabbiness. Quietly, they informed me that the embassy had recently moved to this location because after the numerous coup d'etats in Liberia, the government was unable to afford the proper facilities where the embassy had previously been located.

When we arrived at the embassy office on the third floor, it seemed in worse shape than the hallways. Maintenance workers were trying to clean up the mess left by the previous tenants, while construction workers were tearing down plasterboard walls and doorways. In the midst of all this, people were sitting and waiting for their names to be called in order to enter the embassy's office. Since the official native language of Liberia is English, I felt less intimidated. Mani, carrying Nesya, Dora, and I approached the clerk who seemed to be in charge. We told her that we needed to see the ambassador as soon as possible. She asked us to briefly explain the problem. She did not seem shocked or surprise at what we told her. However, she immediately disappeared into one of the inner offices. When she returned, she said that we would have to meet with the assistant ambassador first, and we would have to come back in the afternoon when the ambassador would be there. Again, we were faced with a situation where we did not have enough time to return to the ULE, and we would have to find a way to occupy our time until our appointment with the ambassador in the afternoon. I felt like I had seen enough deprivation and neglect, and I did not feel like walking up and down the streets, looking for some type of visual entertainment. I opted to sit and wait, while Dora and Mani decided to take Nesya and explore the surroundings. I tried to get comfortable on the armchair whose springs were bulging through the upholstery. I moved to another chair with a vinyl covering, but nails in the chair's back were protruding and snagged my blouse. I rather regretted not having gone out with Dora, Nesya, and Mani. I felt that if time could go any slower, it would be going in reverse. I had to find a way to entertain myself. So, I imagined scenarios for those sitting and waiting in this waiting room. One, I imagined was a dignitary who needed to speak with the ambassador about handling negotiations in Ghana. For a woman, who had several small children with her, I surmised that she was trying to get help in locating her husband who had been drafted into the army. Thus, I occupied my time for the next three hours.

Finally, at about 3:35 p.m., three very distinguish-looking gentlemen, dressed in traditional gowns, entered the waiting room. Everyone jumped up. I did too, even though I did not really know why. These men passed through the waiting room, without acknowledging anyone there. They locked the door behind them after they entered one of the interior offices. Everyone sat down again.

A few minutes later, two more very distinguished looking men, dressed in modern suits entered the embassy. Again, everyone stood up. However, instead of just walking through the waiting room and entering one of the offices, the taller of the two men, greeted the receptionist and several of the people. Each one smiled, bowed their heads, and returned the greeting. Though I was already sitting, he also turned to me and said, "Hello," to which I responded accordingly. Only after the two men left the waiting room and entered one of the inner offices did everyone start chattering discretely about the two men. I overheard one person say that the ambassador was such a fine and distinguished person. From this, I understood that I had just been acknowledged by the Liberian Ambassador. I was really impressed by his demeanor. He was dignified but cordial and respectful.

About ten minutes after his arrival, Mani and Dora returned with Nesya. They had explored the surrounding neighborhood and window-shopped. They suggested that after we left the embassy, all four of us should spend some time, just walking around and taking in the sights. This sounded like a good idea, since most of the time we were always "on business." They asked me if the ambassador had arrived, and I told them that he had. About twenty minutes later, someone brought a document to the receptionist. She looked at it briefly and called out a person's name. Then, she added, "The Ambassador will see you now." Several people were called into the ambassador's office. Afterwards they left the building, most of them with satisfied looks on their faces. Finally, I heard my name called. The four of us, Mani, Dora, Nesya, and I entered the ambassador's office. He asked us about our backgrounds. He paid special attention to Nesya, tickling her and teasing her. Then, he said to me, "I wish there were more people like you who could save our children." This statement caught me by surprise. I was really moved by the fact that the ambassador took such a strong interest in what was happening to the children of Liberia. I thanked him for his kind words. Then, he told me that he would have to review the adoption papers more thoroughly, and that we should return the next day, after they had been certified and stamped with the official seal of the Liberian Embassy.

After we left his office, we sighed with relief. Things seemed to be progressing favorably. A leisurely walk through downtown Abidjan would be salubrious. We stopped and looked in a variety of shop windows. Mani liked looking at the electronic equipment and roaming through the men's clothing store, of which there was an over-abundance. Dora liked looking at the house-ware goods, which were tastefully displayed; but I was not sure who could afford to buy them. As for me, of course, every children's clothing store caught my eye. While we were looking in one store window, I noticed a few people standing around us, staring at us. I was a little startled by this until I understood why "we" had attracted attention. Actually, it was Nesya was attracting all the attention. She was entertaining herself by looking at her reflection in the windows while she danced and sang. She seemed so "professional" at this that even dignified men in suits stopped to see her performance. I was not sure how to respond. Should I just smile with pride, or should I "pass the hat." I whispered to Mani, "Let's get out of here!" Mani picked up Nesya and began to walk on. Dora and I followed them. As we walked, I tried to understand why this little tiny bundle of joy stood out among all the other children. What was so special about her?

The next morning I woke up feeling a strong sense of excitement. I was looking forward to going to the Liberian Embassy to get Nesya's papers. Upon completing our morning routine, we flagged down a taxi and headed towards the embassy. I was filled with expectation as we climbed the stairs to the embassy. The receptionist had already been informed of the purpose of our visit, and she informed the ambassador that we had arrived. Within a few minutes, we were called into his office. He stamped the documents in our presence, placed a tender kiss on Nesya's cheek, and wished us well. I thanked him profusely for his help. He smiled at me and waved to us as we left his office. As we walked out, both Dora and Mani looked at me with satisfaction. Things seemed to be going well. Now, all we had to do was to take the documents to the Israel Embassy.

At eleven o'clock, we arrived at the Israel Embassy. We did not have to wait long before the ambassador called me into his office. He looked through the documents that I handed him, and smiled with satisfaction. "At least this part is taken care of," he said. "I'll send these documents to Israel. It might be a few days before we get a response, but I will notify you as soon as we hear from them. However, the Child Welfare Services wants an additional document. They want a signed and certified statement from Nesya's biological mother, stating the name's of her (the mother's) parents and what village they are from." While I was still pondering the reason for this strange request, he added, "And they want a signed affidavit from the mother, stating that she will never try to make contact with Nesya, and she will never try to come to Israel." Though, maybe I should not have been surprised at this request, I still was shocked at the harshness of such a request. Then, the most agonizing request was made. "A visa will be granted in three days if you can get these documents to me within that time. Otherwise, the authorities in Israel (i.e. Child Welfare) will oppose any effort to take the child to Israel." I felt totally numb. I could not comprehend what was happening. I just sat there for a moment. When I regained my senses, I thanked the ambassador and left his office.

When I stepped into the hallway, Dora and Mani could tell that something was wrong. I told them what had transpired in the ambassador's office. Dora stood opposite me with a look of disbelief. Mani was standing with his back to us. When he turned around, I saw tears streaming down his cheeks. Then, he began to share with us what he had suffered in trying to get Nesya's adoption approved in Liberia. Nesya's mother lived in a village several hours from the capitol, Monrovia. Mani had traveled there to take Nesya and her mother to Monrovia to the court to submit the adoption request. After that, he traveled back to the village with them and, then, returned to Monrovia to oversee the adoption process. He also had to take Nesya to Monrovia for medical tests to be sure she was healthy. Several times, under rulings from the court, he had to travel to the village and back to Monrovia. On one of these trips he was captured by rebel soldiers, who are *not* noted for their kindness. They interrogated him and searched his body thoroughly. At one point, one of the soldiers stuck his hand in Mani's left shirt pocket and pulled out an army cap. This cap was not a Liberian army cap. *It was an Israeli army cap!* Mani had spent several years in Israel, working with the elderly; this was his profession. He had warm feelings for Israel, and as a souvenir he had bought an army cap, which he always kept over his heart in his left shirt pocket. The soldier looked at him with a malicious grin, and then he said one of the most outrageous sentences that could be imagined. "Because of the Israelis we are in turmoil in our country!" (Even in the interior of Africa's heartland, Israel was being blamed!) After declaring this absurdity, Mani was beaten and tortured and thrown into a pit with thousands of red ants, who wasted no time in attacking him from every angle. It was only a miracle that he was able to escape and that he survived. From then on, when he had to travel to the village, he chose to walk along the railroad tracks which were covered with tall weeds. These tracks had not been used since the coup d'etat in Liberia twelve years earlier, when all public utilities had been destroyed. Upon concluding his horrific story, Mani said quietly, "I gave my life for this child. Now, they want me to risk my life again."

We left the embassy office in silence. The day before it seemed that we were near the end of the obstacles standing between us and Israel, and, now, today an obstacle the size of a glacier was looming in front of us. As we rode back to Riveria Place, we noticed the increase military movement on the roads. We were all well aware that another "coup" was pending, and I knew that I had to notify people back home of the seriousness of the situation. In addition to this, I had to find a way to get the necessary papers to get the visa. When we arrived at Rachel's, everyone was excited to hear what we had accomplished at the Israel Embassy. I cannot remember who spoke first, but I do remember the looks on the residents' faces. Their looks ranged from total shock to great fear. Then, everyone began giving their opinion about how we could surmount this mountain of impediment, which had many underlying complications, such as:

1) How to notify the mother of what was required from her

2) How to get her to a place where she could draft the letter and have it typed

3) How to get the letter authorized in Liberia

4) How to get the letter sent to Abidjan within three days

5) How to get it authenticated by the Liberian Embassy within the
remaining time limit

6) How to get it to the Israel Embassy in time for it to be sent to Israel

Rachel stood at one side of the room. She was deep in thought. Finally, she contributed her ideas. "Well, I have friends who work in the Red Cross in Liberia. If we can get a letter to them, they should be able to get it to the mother in the village. If it is signed in front of them, they can put a stamp of veracity on it and take it to the courthouse in Monrovia. From there, it can be faxed to Abidjan, and we can handle it from this point." Everyone clapped and cheered at her brilliant idea. Then someone reminded us that first we had to get the letter ready and fax it to Liberia in order to get the ball rolling. At this point, there was a communal sigh of desperation. Then I said, "If there is a typewriter handy, I can compose the letter to be faxed to Liberia." Again, there were cheers and applause. Dora walked slowly to the corner of the room near the large living room window, bent down and lifted up an old fashioned Royal typewriter, the kind that was used during World War II. She gently placed it on the dining room table in front of me. The keys were black and encased in gold metal frames. The ribbon was well worn, and when the keys were struck, they stuck to the ribbon, so every time I struck a key, I had to manually place it in its original position. I saw that I had my work cut out for me. First, I wrote out the letter by hand. I rewrote it several times so that there would not be room for misunderstanding or error. I did not want Child Welfare to find in fault with the declaration requested and consider it null- and- void. I rewrote the letter so many times that my fingers began to ache. Finally, after what seemed like hours, I was satisfied with the format of the letter, and I began typing it on "ole Mr. Royal." I wasn't exactly doing "touch-typing," but rather "plunk-and-pull" typing. When I was composing the letter, only my right hand hurt, but now that I was trying to type it, both of my hands hurt, and my wrist also hurt. In addition to "plunk-and-pull," if I made a mistake, I had to erase it, carefully, in order not to tear the paper, and then, re-type the word. All the while, I was aware of the ticking of the huge wall clock. I had to finish the letter before four o'clock so that we could take it down the street and around the corner to the shop where faxes were sent. If we did not make it to the shop before it closed, we would have to wait to the next day in order to send it. The pressure made me make more mistakes as I got near the end of the letter. I was covered with sweat by the time I finished it. As soon as I took it out of the typewriter, Mani snatched it from my hand, and shouted, "Let's go!" We left Nesya with Rachel, ran out of the apartment, down the four flights of stairs, through the parking lot , down to the main street, crossed it, and hurried passed the "rib joint" to the fax shop. We got there 15 minutes before it closed. We stood in line behind seven other people who were waiting to send faxes. I prayed that our experience with this shop would not be like the French Embassy or the photo shop, and promptly at four o'clock the shop would be closed and we would be left with the letter still in our hand. I nervously shook my right leg as if a cock roach was climbing up it. At two minutes before four o'clock, it was our turn to present our fax. The clerk dialed the fax number, but it was busy. He tried again, and it was still busy. We knew that Rachel had planned to call her friends at the Red Cross and tell them what to expect, but we did not know if the fax phone at the Red Cross was the same phone for regular calls. I looked at the wall clock; it was exactly four o'clock.

However, the clerk did not stop trying. At 4:07, the fax finally went through! What a relief! Instead of leaving the office, I plopped myself down on one of the seats. I was totally exhausted. The office workers were very polite and let me sit for a few minutes. When I regained my strength, I stood up and we returned to Rachel's. She had successfully notified her friends, and they said that as soon as they got the letter they would head out towards the village. I was struck by the thought of what had happened to Mani when he traveled along the main road to the village. I hoped there would be no problems for these angels of mercy on the way there.

My body and soul were ravaged by the stress and uncertainty of the predicament I was in. I lay in bed and wrote my friend, Leah, a letter about what was happening. (Note: "the Griot" – pronounced "gree-yo", is an African equivalent to "Murphey's Law.")

Dear Leah,

Well, the Griot has got me. I went to the Israel Embassy today, and they gave me the list of things the Jerusalem office has required of me before the visa will be issued:

1) Full name of Nesya's biological mother
2) Full names of Nesya's biological mother's parents
3) Nesya's mother's birth certificate or passport number or I.D. number
4) Place of birth and date of birth of Nesya's biological mother
5) A letter from her biological mother signed by her, stating that she will *never* visit or try to visit Israel
6) The above letter must be certified by a lawyer or notary public (notarion)
7) A letter from me stating everything I know about Nesya's biological mother

. . . . . . and all this must be done by Thursday, three days from now!

HaShem yerahem! (i.e. "L-rd have mercy!")

Chapter Eight

THE SWISS EMBASSY

Time was running out, and I felt desperate. I had to find a way to get home. Things were not progressing well, and I was still caught in a muddle of bureaucracy. A meeting was called at the ULE in Rachel's house. Everyone gave his idea about how to proceed. We went through the list of embassies we had approached and their responses. It was time to approach the other embassies, and as planned, we decided to go to the Swiss Air office and the Swiss Embassy. We had to verify that there were direct flights from Abidjan to Israel. We also had to verify if a transit visa was required. Rachel called the Swiss Air office so that I could book a flight. They were not accepting phone reservations. That meant we had to take a taxi for what seemed like the one hundredth time to downtown Abidjan.

After making several wrong turns, we arrived at Swiss Air, located on an extremely beautiful contoured boulevard. It was here that we had once changed money on the black market. Several men, some well-dressed and some in simple work uniforms, stood at strategic points, opposite the modern office buildings. Other men, who seemed to be less affluent, were walking casually among the leafy foliage in the center of the boulevard. They, too, were waiting for "customers" to approach them. The exchange was done discreetly, with various disguises to avoid the eyes of the police who were cruising the area – though I am sure that the police knew exactly what was going on.

Inside the Swiss Air office there were lines of people waiting for their number to be called. After waiting for nearly an hour, our number was called. We explained to the clerk that I wanted to fly to Israel with my adopted daughter. I needed to know about visa requirements for us before I bought a ticket. The clerk looked intently at her computer screen, while pressing keys in search of the necessary information. There was no clear answer. She checked with her immediate supervisor, who checked with her supervisor, who speculated that a visa was needed, and we would have to go to the Swiss Embassy. We requested that the supervisor call the embassy to find out what were the rules and regulations. (We were trying to avoid an unnecessary trip.) After waiting for more than 45 minutes, while the clerks and supervisors tried to contact the embassy, it became clear that we would have to go in person to the embassy. The clerk said that the embassy was within walking distance, and it was, but there was one major inconvenience. All the streets and sidewalks in the area were undergoing repair. We had to jump over ditches, crisscross the streets several times in order to navigate our way around the construction work. My legs began to ache as I pulled my feet from the sand dunes piled beside the ditches. When we finally got to the embassy building, we discovered that the office we needed was on the third floor. Needless to say, we were all out of breath when we arrived.

The embassy office was _**very**_ modest – almost stark. The staff was nearly as stark as their office. Their smiles were cool and controlled. I told the attending clerk that I wanted to fly Swiss Air to Israel, but since there were no direct flights, I would have to fly through Zurich. I needed to know if I needed a visa for myself and for my daughter. She asked to see our passports. Because of the differences in our passports, I immediately handed her Nesya's adoption papers. She scrutinized them for a long time. Then, she said she would have to show them to her superior. I was afraid to let our documents out of my sight, but I did not know how to avoid it. She disappeared into one of the inner rooms. I felt a little less nervous when I could hear their muffled voices. At least the documents were not far away. Several minutes later, she re-appeared. She informed me that we did, indeed, need visas, but we could not be issued a visa without first having purchased airline tickets. I felt a prick of frustration, thinking about the long walk back and forth between the airline office and the embassy.

With documents in hand, we all headed back to the airline office. It was slightly easier because we had learned where the roughest points were along the way, and we could avoid them. The ticket agent was quite congenial. She did not make us wait in line again. Another clerk took our papers to the cashier and processed them. This gave us a few more minutes to sit and rest. With tickets in hand, we made our way back to the Swiss Embassy. Fortunately, Nesya had not been fretful while being jostled about over hill and dale. She seemed to enjoy the outing. Perched in her backpack carrier, she sang and pointed at objects which attracted her attention. Still, it was a difficult trek, trying to carry her, either in our arms or in the backpack. We had trouble keeping our balance. At one point, I almost fell in a ditch. Mani took her out of the carrier and carried her in his arms. He, too, slipped while trying to balance his jiggling bundle. Nesya seemed to think that it was amusing.

Once back at the embassy, we had to wait in line again. Eleven people stood in front of us. Dora sat with Nesya, changed her diaper, and fed her. The line moved slowly. The two clerks at the desk did their job with exactness. I heard one clerk say to the applicants that their visas would be ready in two weeks! I had been in Abidjan for nearly three weeks, and I dreaded the thought of having to extend my stay for another two weeks. Well, if it meant that then this ordeal would come to an end, I would find the strength to endure. Finally, it was my turn. I presented my papers, along with the airline tickets. The clerk again scrutinized them thoroughly, and again she took them into the inner office to her superior. When she returned, the little civility which she had had in her composure had totally disappeared. She handed me my documents and tickets and curtly stated, "We cannot grant you a visa." I waited for her to explain "why," but she gave no further explanation. So, I asked for an explanation. "We have no proof that your documents are legal." "But these are the original documents, with the state seals," I exclaimed. With a piercing look, she scowled, "We have no way of verifying this." "All I want to do is take my baby home, home to Israel!" My voice began to crack. I knew I would no longer be able to hold back the tears. Tears streamed down my face. The clerk looked at me coolly and said, "Well, you can take your baby home, but not through Switzerland." She seemed to enjoy making this statement. I got up, stood in the middle of the room, looked at her squarely in the eyes and shouted, "Heil Hitler!", while I imitated the Nazi salute. She was so startled she jumped. Fear nearly overcame her. She tried to regain her composure as best she could as she retorted, "Heil Hitler!" However, she did not salute because her hand was reaching for the emergency button underneath the counter. I knew she was alerting the police or the security guards. I sat down in one of the chairs in the waiting room, and I stared relentlessly at her every move. It was obvious that I had unnerved her. She fiddled with papers, not really knowing what she was doing. She went into one of the side offices and spoke with her superior. He did not come out. She came out and pretended she was looking for documents. I did not remove my glare from her ghost-white face. Every now and then, she would look at the huge wall clock. At exactly one-thirty- closing time, with great restraint she said we must leave. I did not budge. Her face showed signs of controlled rage. She began to demand loudly that we leave. Realizing that any further delay or confrontation would not be beneficial, I slowly stood up, and the four of us exited the premises.

Silently, we walked back to the Swiss Air office. I am not sure what Mani and Dora were thinking or what they thought of my actions at the embassy office, but I felt a sense of *release.* It was hard living under such stress for such a long period of time. When we entered the Swiss Air office, the clerks were surprised to see us. We told them that the embassy had refused to grant us visas. They looked dumbfounded. All of us were wondering what had been the purpose of having me buy the tickets, if they were not going to issue visas. Most of the staff whispered among themselves and looked embarrassed. With apologetic gestures, the tickets were cancelled and my money was returned to me.

Upon leaving the airline office, we repeated our almost daily routine. We flagged down a taxi and told the driver to take us to Riveria Place. As was her custom, Nesya immediately fell asleep in my arms. All of us rested our heads on the back of the seat. We were too tired to think and too tired to talk. Rain began to pelt the taxi's windows. Soon, the streets were washed with rain. Abidjan looked quite different while it was raining. A song from my childhood came into my head. "Over my head there is music in the air. There must be G-d somewhere." To me, rain signified that G-d was still in control. No situation is static. G-d can be found in the midst of our sorrow. He **never** deserts us. We must always keep our channels of communication with Him open.

As if by instinct, when we arrived at Rachel's door, she immediately opened it for us. I looked at her, and she stared back at me. "I need a hug," I said, and we stood and embraced each other. This hug transcended all earthly divisions among people. It was a "sister" hug, a hug that extended back more than 250 years, when African families were torn apart by slavery. It was a hug that said, "I share your pain."

Another Shabbat was approaching. I looked in the cardboard box at the head of my bed to see what I could come up with to eat on Shabbat. I found two tins of sardines and a can of corn. This was a far cry from what I was used to having in Israel on Shabbat, but I decided not to let that thought put me in a bad mood. I had to create the Sabbath atmosphere as best as I could. I rummaged through the cardboard box again, and I found a small bottle of grape juice, the kind which is given on Purim. Ah! This would make my/our Shabbat special. Rachel had some nice white paper napkins, which contrasted well with the white lace table cloth, which always covered the dining room table. I placed the napkins beside the blue plastic plates and cups which I had bought. The color combination was reminiscent of the flag of Israel. After having set the table, I bathed Nesya and dressed her in one of the two dresses she had. Then, I put large white ribbons on her little tufts of hair and sat her in the high chair opposite the television, to keep her entertained while I bathed and dressed for the Shabbat. Television was always on because everyone wanted to keep abreast of the news, since it was obvious that the country was on the verge of another "coup." When I went back to the living room, Mani was sitting on the floor with Nesya swaying back and forth on his left knee. He was playing a hand game with her, while he kept glancing at the television to listen to the news. I took this opportunity to light candles to initiate the Sabbath and begin the evening prayers. Because of the noise from the television, I had to concentrate deeply on the words of the prayers. As I was saying them, I looked for solacement. The intensity of this concentration seemed to transport me back to Israel, to Hevron (Hebron), to the Tomb of the Patriarchs, to "Me'arat HaMachpela." I remember the sound of the footsteps on the winding stone paths which lead to the "Me'ara." The sound echoes off the stone buildings nestled in the valley in which the cave is located. There are several paths leading to the Me'ara, which can only be seen when at the point where the paths converge. Hundreds of people come to the Me'ara on Shabbat Eve. Young boys, youth, and men of all ages have the custom of wearing white, especially white shirts on the Sabbath Eve. Their attire gives the appearance of angels descending into the valley surrounding the Me'ara. Soon afterwards, mothers with small children and babies, women, and young girls from Hevron and from Kiryat Arba begin their trek to down the paths to the Me'ara. The Sabbath greeting, "Shabbat Shalom," is exchanged among all those going to pray. The atmosphere is of a collective heart, beating with excitement. This joy and excitement intensifies about three minutes before making the last turn, after which the Me'ara becomes visible, in all its glory. My heart always skips a beat when I reach this point. I pause for a moment to take in the unique sight of the Me'ara, crowned in the golden rays of the setting sun. All those who approach the Me'ara are well aware that they are about to enter one of the most holy sites on earth. The term "Me'ara" means cave in Hebrew. Underneath the majestic edifice which we call "Me'arat HaMachpela" (i.e. The Cave of the Pairs/ Couples) are the burial sites of Avraham and Sara, Yitzhak (Issac) and Rivka (Rebecca), and Ya'acov (Jacob) and Leah. Further inside the cave, Adam, and his wife Chava (Eve) are buried. One cannot help feeling the connection with our forefathers and living biblical history.

As the hundreds of worshippers ascend the steps to the Me'ara, there is a pulsating in the frontal lobes of our brains. Once inside the building, every antechamber and the central courtyard are filled with Jews, who chant the prayer melodies according to the customs of their ancestors. The European melodies mingle with those of the Yemenite tradition. The Moroccan melodies soar high and blend with the vigorous Carlebach melodies. The words of all the prayers are 90% the same, consisting of passages from the Bible and poetry written hundreds of years ago. Jews are very strong on keeping tradition, and the tunes in which they sing the prayers allow for freedom of personal inspiration. I am totally encompassed by the song "Yedid Nefesh."

The words of this poem/song refer to G-d as our sincerest, closest and most intimate friend, our merciful father, with Whom the connection is so strong that we run to be close to Him and do His will The joy of doing His will is like the sweet taste of honey. We ask G-d to cover us with His love and His protection. I inhaled deeply so that the special odor of the Me'ara could fill my lungs. With each breath I took, the fragrance of the Me'ara and the strength of the words of the song permeated my whole being, and I knew I would overcome every obstacle and return to Israel with Nesya, and we would be able to celebrate at the Me'ara.

At this point, I slowly returned to my present state. I went to the living room and lifted Nesya into my arms and sat her in the high chair, to celebrate with me the Sabbath meal. For the rest of the Shabbat, I tried to maintain the atmosphere which I had created through my evening prayers. And, thus, was my second Sabbath away from home. I now had enough strength to deal with the new week's pending ordeals. Tomorrow, I would be alone with Nesya, while the residents of ULE spent their day in church.

. . . .

This Sunday began as the previous one had. All the members of the ULE put on their Sunday apparel and went to church. Since they would be there most of the day, I could spend quality time with Nesya. After they left, I put Nesya in the large blue basin and let her splash to her heart's content. Then, I dried her, dressed her, and sat her in the bedroom near the bathroom door. That way I could keep an eye on her while I sat on the wooden stool with my feet in the blue basin.

Afterwards, I prepared our two meals for the day. This was quite a procedure since I had only two pots, and the stove had only one burner which was dependable. The second burner was temperamental and worked only when it felt like it. After succeeding in preparing the food, I then, had to find a space in the refrigerator to store it. The refrigerator was quite small, and it barely kept food cold. On the outer side of the wall where the refrigerator stood, I could hear the rats scurrying about, near the kitchen window. I cautiously peered out the window, afraid to find a rat staring back at me and my freshly cooked food. I breathed a little easier when I did not see a big fat gray rat sitting on the window ledge.

With breakfast ready, we sat down at the oval dining-room table adjacent to the television. Nesya had learned to use the remote control. She flipped back and forth through the four or five channels which were available. On all them, there were choirs singing. Some choirs had only women singing. Some choirs wore identical choir robes, while others sufficed with wearing dresses of the same color. However, all the choir members had the bright-colored scarves tied to their wrists. They raised and lowered the scarves as they sang and swayed in time with the music.

After about seven choirs sang, there was a news break and a brief review of the day's programs. Since the news was in French, I could only surmise what was being said by looking at the accompanying pictures. Today, however, certain words drew my attention, and I tried very hard to understand what was being said. I thought I heard Israel mentioned. I strained to understand more. It seemed that they were saying something about children who were being taken from Abidjan and smuggled into Israel! Could this be?! My French was so poor that I was certain that I had misunderstood. I did, however, feel a bit worried. I changed channels. I found a program about village life, showing how food was prepared over open fires outside the huts. Barefooted children smiled shyly into the camera. I tried to imagine the type of village my daughter was from. She, too, had not worn shoes until her uncle had bought her a pair before they boarded a plane to meet me. It was hard to tell which of the children were boys and which were girls because their hair was cropped short. Nesya had sparse patches of hair about a quarter of an inch long. She did, however, look like a girl – maybe, because her ears had been pierced. Now she had tiny gold loop earrings which Rachel had bought her, but when she was first put in my arms, she only had small pieces of an unidentifiable metal looped through her ears. I wondered if her biological mother had done that in order to make her more attractive or more presentable. I sighed heavily at the thought of what had transpired before the mother put Nesya in Mani's arms, kissed her gently, and watched them walk away. I went over to Nesya, picked her up and hugged her – a hug for me and a hug for her other mother.

At 3:30 p.m., all the residents of ULE returned, bringing a few more guests. I wondered how many of these guests would soon become residents of ULE. Her apartment was actually a refugee shelter as well as a transit stop. In 1990's, there had been a coup d'etat in Liberia. It was brutal and savage. Dams had been bombed, leaving even major cities without electricity and running water. Until today, only a few families can afford a generator to supply electricity, but most people have to wait for trucks to deliver water and milk products. Thousands of people were killed in that war and many more became refugees in neighboring countries. The refugee population was a burden to the local population, and they were made to feel so. They were the last to be hired and the first to be fired. Though color-wise they blended in, something in their demeanor, manner of speech and dress made them stand out as "foreigners." Rachel had managed to survive in Abidjan for ten years. Though she had a fairly good job, her pay was less than that of a native citizen. Still, on her meager salary, she provided food for everyone who knew about her apartment and used it as a way-station, whether for a day or two or for several weeks. She knew how and where to shop to get the best bargains. She and Dora carried up those several flights of stairs kilos upon kilos of fruit, fish, and vegetables, and 20 kilo sacks of rice. I thought of her as truly a righteous gentile.

After the crowd had had their Sunday meal, as was their routine, they moved to the sofa and chairs to listen to the news. Today, there were so many guests that some had to sit on the floor. The news started as usual, with the military government trying to use psychological cunning to keep the people under control. Later on in the news, I heard Israel mentioned again. The newscaster seemed to be repeating what I had heard earlier. During a commercial break, I asked Rachel to tell me what was said about Israel. She hesitated for a moment and then said, "International agencies are concerned that Abidjan is being used as a transport center to smuggle African children, including many Liberian children, to Israel before they are shipped to other countries, especially to European countries. The agencies are not sure whether the children have been kidnapped or sold by their parents, or if their parents are trying to smuggle them out in order to give them a chance of survival." Rachel was quiet. I stood dumbfounded. We were probably thinking the same thing. "So, this was the reason I was having trouble getting a visa for Nesya. Here I was, trying to leave Abidjan to go to Israel with a Liberian child!" How could this unfortunate chain-of-events be happening at this exact time! Now, I understood better what had transpired at the Swiss Embassy!

Chapter Nine

Salvation Sunday

Repetition can be monotonous or it can be comforting. I had almost begun to enjoy the quiet repetition of each Sunday. I enjoyed the time I could be alone with my daughter. I had lay in bed with Nesya until the residents of ULE had left for church. Then, I got up to prepare Nesya's breakfast, which consisted of porridge and fruit-flavored yogurts. While I was doing so, Nesya played with the remote control of the television, flipping from channel to channel. By the time she finished eating breakfast, it was nearly noon. It would be hours before the residents would return to have their Sunday meal. I contemplated venturing out to the nearby open-air market and to continue on to a small strip of shops where the pharmacy was located. That side of the neighborhood made me feel uncomfortable, for at the end of the street was the line of "demarcation" – the walls that separated the "have-nots" from the "haves." On the other side of those walls were the spacious villas of the wealthy. I never saw anyone go in or out of the villas, but it was easy to tell from the landscaping around the high security gates that the occupants of those villas were not simple "locals." These homes were probably owned by foreign investors, of which Africa had many. Unfortunately, the investments stopped at the security gates and did not trickle down to the average citizen. The only thing the two sides of the walls had in common were the huge palm trees and lush foliage that seemed to sprout up to defy the boundaries.

As I was enjoying the view from the living-room window, the doorbell rang, intruding on my serenity. This bell was the only thing, which seemed to be the only thing in the apartment which worked properly. Since it was too early for the residents to be returning home, I approached the door cautiously and asked who was there. One of the people gave a name which sounded familiar; so, I opened the door. Indeed it was one of the residents, and with her were two other women, one of which she introduced as their minister. They entered the living room and sat down. Angela (the temporary resident) informed the others that I was from Israel. The minister acted as if she was surprised, but I was sure that she had been briefed about my background. "Oh!," she said, trying to sound surprised. "I would love to hear about Israel. Could you, please, tell us about Israel." Trying to continue in her polite tone, I asked, "Well, what would you like to know – about the people or the culture or the tourists' sites?" Maintaining her polite tone, she replied, "Oh, I would like to know about the holy sites and specifically about the Jewish religion. Sensing where this conversation was going, I asked, "Which do you want to know more about, the holy sites or the Jewish religion?" "Actually, I would like to know more about the Jewish beliefs." Having had experience with missionaries, my radar went up. I knew exactly what she was trying to get to. Without hesitating, I said bluntly, "Let's be honest. You want to save my soul, and I want to stay as I am." She was caught off guard by my bluntness. "Well, maybe, you could help me understand what you people believe." Her voice was less patronizing now. "All right," I replied. "Then, take out your bible." All three pulled their bibles from their handbags.

"Let's start with Genesis 1:1." We read through the days of creation and paused when we got to the passage about Shabbat. "And what happened on the seventh day," I asked. "G-d rested," the minister replied. "So, when is your day of rest?" I asked. She paused for a moment. "Well, there are reasons for that," she retorted. "There are reasons which override what G-d has commanded?," I probed.

"Before we get into more biblical polemics, let's take a step back and look at the Foundation of Humanity – that is mutual respect. I respect you as a human being. I also respect your right to believe in any form of super-power that you choose. As a member of the human race, you are obligated to respect me as a human being and also my right to believe in whatever higher power I choose. This is the Foundation of Humanity.

We have seen in the past how zealousness for religious beliefs has caused mayhem and havoc in society. We have only to look back to the year 1096 C.E., when the first crusaders set out for the Holy Land, in an attempt to regain claim over it from the Muslim conquerors. How many people were killed in this crusade and the subsequent crusades, which continued until the 1300's? The last crusade was the Children's Crusade. How many children died as a result of starvation, exposure to the elements, or drowning? How many of those children who survived these ordeals were sold into slavery because of someone's religious fervor? The initial raison d'etre was to uproot the Islamic control over the Holy Land. This soon became a camouflage for pillaging, looting, and conquering whatever stood in their way. For two hundred years, Christians and Moslems fought each other to gain territory, and they often used force to spread their religions. Yet, both groups accepted the Ten Commandments as tenets of their faith. As you are well aware, "Thou shall not kill" is one of the Ten Commandments. Though today, the crusades are being conducted in a less violent way, the ideology is still the same - to try to influence or change someone's religious beliefs. The underlying factor is religious zeal. "Zealotry" is a reflexive action, meant to bring internal joy and satisfaction to a person. It is *not* meant to be a "transitive" action. When zeal is stretched beyond an intransitive level, it creates anarchy and it violates the Foundation of Humanity.

A second point I would like to address is the question of why most Jews do not participate in inter-faith dialogue. It is not because we are afraid, nor that we have something to hide or be ashamed of. It is because Jews and non-Jews have different points of reference, which do not correlate. You see, without a good knowledge of Hebrew, non-Jews are greatly limited in their ability to understand where Jews are "coming from" in terms of religious beliefs. Christians make assumptions about Judaism based mainly on their understanding of Matthew, Mark, Luke, and John. This is equivalent to arriving late (about 2,000 years late) to a movie theater featuring "The History of Mankind," and according to what is on the screen at the moment, making assumptions about what happened during the previous scenes that were missed. At this point, I cannot brief you on the 2,000 years that you missed. However, I can give you a thumb-nail sketch of a Jew's connection with their Creator. Now, let's continue where we left off in our search for understanding the Jew and his connection with G-d."

Genesis 13: 14 -17

And the Eternal said to Avram (i.e. Abraham), after Lot had departed from him, "Lift up your eyes, and look from the place where you are now, northward, southward, eastward, and westward, for all the land which you see, to you I will give it and to your seed (i.e. offspring) ***forever***."

Let's move on to the Book of Exodus:

Exodus 30: 8

And when Aaron set up the lamps at even, he shall cause them to ascend in fumes, a perpetual incense before the Eternal ***throughout your generations***.

Exodus 30: 21

They (Aaron, the priest, and his sons) shall wash their hands and their feet, that they will not die, and it shall be a statute (i.e. law) ***forever*** to them, even to him and his seed, ***throughout their generations***.

Exodus 30: 30, 31

And you (Moses) shall anoint Aaron and his sons, and sanctify them, that they may minister unto Me as priests. And you shall speak to the children of Israel, saying, "this shall be an oil of anointment to Me, ***throughout your generations***."

Exodus 31: 12, 13

And the Eternal spoke to Moses, saying, "Speak to the children of Israel, saying, "Verily, my Sabbaths you shall keep: for it is a sign between Me and you *__throughout your generations__*, that you

Exodus 31: 16, 17

Therefore, the children of Israel shall keep the Sabbath, to observe the Sabbath *__throughout their generations__* for a covenant *__forever__*. It is a sign between Me and the children of Israel *__forever__*: for in six days the Eternal made heaven and earth, and on the seventh day He rested and was refreshed.

There is one common thread throughout *__all__* of these passages. G-d made a commitment to His people, *__forever, throughout all their generations__*. We will find this same precept throughout the Bible, but let's look at two more passages from the Book of Deuteronomy:

Deuteronomy 11: 1

Therefore, you shall love the Eternal, your G-d, and keep His charge, and His laws, and His judgments, and His commandments, *__always.__*

Deuteronomy 11: 18 -22

Therefore, you shall put these, My words, in your heart and in your soul, and bind them for a sign upon your hand,

and they shall be as frontlets between your eyes. And you shall teach them to your children, speaking of them while you are sitting in your house, and while you are walking on your way, and while you are lying down, and when you get up. And you shall write them upon the door-posts of your house and on your gates. That your days may increase, and the days of your children, on the ground which the Eternal swore unto your fathers to give them, as the days of heaven upon the earth.

The Creator did not put a time limit on His covenant with His people. We, the Jewish people are committed to Him, and He is committed to us, *__forever.__*

As far as sin and atonement are concerned, we need to look at the Book of Exodus and the Book of Leviticus:

Exodus 20: 1 -6

And the Eternal spoke all these words, saying, "I am the Eternal thy G-d, who brought you out of the land of Egypt, out of the house of servants. You shall have no other gods before my face. You shall not make for yourselves any graven image, or any likeness of *__any thing__* that is in the heavens above, or that is in the earth beneath, or that is in the water under the earth. For, I, the Eternal your G-d, am a jealous G-d, visiting the sins of the fathers upon the children unto the third and fourth generation of them that hate Me, and (I) show mercy *__for thousands of generations__* to those who love Me.

From these verses you can see that *__even__* when Jews sinned, the Creator did *__not__* punish His people forever. So, the concept of "original sin" could in no way be passed down throughout all the generations. Therefore, you, as Christians, do not need to "save" us.

So, what happens when a Jew does sin, as everyone does? G-d took this into consideration, and showed us how to atone and correct the situation. He provided several ways to accomplish this. I will limit myself to two more examples:

Exodus 30: 15, 16

The rich shall not give more, and the indigent shall not give less than the half of a shekel, in giving a heave offering unto the Eternal, to make an expiation for your souls. And you (Moses) shall take the expiation money from the children of Israel, and shall give it for the service of the appointed tent, that it may be a memorial unto the children of Israel before the Eternal, to make an expiation for your souls.

Leviticus 23: 26 -28, 31

And the Eternal spoke to Moses, saying, "Therefore, on the tenth day of the seventh month, there shall be a day of expiation; it shall be a convocation of holiness for you, and you shall fast and offer a fire offering unto the Eternal. And you shall not do any work on that day, for it is a day of expiation, to make an expiation for you before the Eternal, your G-d." . . . ."You shall not do any work; it shall be an ordinance *__forever, throughout your generations, in all your habitations.__*"

"Every year, we have a special day, Yom Kippur (i.e. the Day of Atonement) which is the culmination of a 10-day period, during which we do intense circumspection, in order to improve ourselves, as we look ahead to the future. I hope this gives you some insight into the soul of the Jewish people.

There are other issues which were brought up today, besides the tenacity of the Jewish people to continue to fulfill G-d's laws. One of the points that was brought up was that non-Jews, or Christians had to be grafted in to the tree of life in order to inherit salvation. My question is 'How can you be grafted in, if you have cut the tree down at its trunk and obliterated its roots?' It was also stated that because Jews are a stiff-necked people, G-d blinded them to the truth, in order to make salvation possible to non-Jews. Basically, what you are saying is that G-d changed the rules of the game while Jews were still on the playing field. He deliberately tricked His people! And He did this so that He could enter into a covenant with a different group of people. Frankly, the Jewish G-d has more integrity than that."

At this point, there was silence, and the "discussion" ended. The minister and her two "disciples" each busied themselves with something else. Shortly afterwards, the rest of the Sunday crew arrived, and they began to prepare for their Sabbath meal. I took Nesya and went to our room and thought about the confrontation.

Chapter Ten

The Coup D'etat

It was about 3 a.m., and I lay in the narrow youth bed with Nesya snuggled up beside me. In the distance, I heard a sound which was hard to distinguish. A few minutes later, I heard more sounds, but this time they were louder and definitely distinguishable. It was gunfire! The "coup" had begun! It seemed that no one else in the apartment heard it. If they did, they were probably lying in bed, wondering what to do. The gunfire became more rapid, and it seemed to becoming from an area that was closer to Riveria Place. For some reason, I was not afraid – maybe, because after having lived in Kiryat-Arba-Hevron, the sound of gunshots had become almost a background noise. So, I lay in bed and waited to see how things would transpire. Then, I started to doze, but the sound of hand-grenades exploding jarred my "tranquility." At this point everyone in the apartment was on their feet, running from room to room to see if all the residents were awake and aware of what was happening. (How could we not be.) Rachel turned on the radio. At first, there was only silence, and then, a lot of static. (Was "no news, good news?!) At around 4:30 a.m., the telephone rang. It was Rachel's boss. Rachel was told that obviously she would not have to report to work at the International School. Luckily, the "coup" had started in the middle of the night, and not as the previous one had, during the day. It had been horrific for the children to be barricaded in bomb shelters or classrooms, each child crying and in a panic, while their frightened teachers, tried to calm them and keep order. Their attempts of re-assurance had little effect, especially since the children's parents were not able to contact them because they were in their respective embassy offices, working frantically to try to obtain information about how serious the situation was, and trying to inform and update their government offices back home. This hellish nightmare continued for three days, until finally the parents were able to contact their children. In the current situation, Rachel's supervisor was reviewing with her, what would be expected of her. However, before he could fully brief her, the phone line went dead. She tried repeatedly to call out, but to no avail. Every time she picked up the phone, it sounded like the line was open, and she could hear faint breathing. She hung up the phone and said quietly, "The line is being tapped." At about 6:00 a.m., there was a loud explosion outside, and it seemed to shake the whole building. Everyone stopped in his tracks. Then, all of a sudden, torrential rain began to pelt the building. The "explosion" was a cloud burst. Everyone gave a sigh of relief and laughed nervously. Myla, one of the house guests, decided to try to use the phone to find out what was happening across town, in a neighborhood where she had relatives. This time, there were no strange sounds on the line; the phone was just dead. We wondered if all the phone lines had purposely been shut down.

With no way of communicating with the outside world, there was nothing much to do, except wait. As had been our morning ritual, Nesya woke up, stretched her arms out to me so that I would pick her up, wash her hands and face, and take her to watch the sunrise. She looked at me quizzically when I just sat with her on the sofa and fed her

her bottle. She pointed towards the window. "Not today, sweety, not today." Everyone knew that in times like this, it was best to stay away from windows. My head was full of all kinds of thoughts:

- How long would the "coup" last?
- How long would we be confined to the apartment with our supplies dwindling?
- How long would we be without any form of communication with the outside world?
- Would the "coup" spread to this area of the city?
- Would people be kidnapped from their homes?

Another thing that worried me was that, fortunately or unfortunately, the day before the coup d'etat, I had received $500 from abroad. Money that was wired from abroad could only be received in the local currency, which I feared would be worthless. If this were to happen, I would be severely limited.

While I was still pondering how to maneuver, the phone rang. All of us nearly jumped out of our skins. Everyone stared at Rachel as if they were circus clowns frozen in time. Only their eyes followed her as she went to answer the phone. The conversation was in French, which I had long since been able to comprehend. Anyway, I was sure it had nothing to do with me. All eyes continued to be focused on her as she conducted the conversation. Then, I heard my name mentioned. Rachel called to me and said, "It's for you." I was too stunned to move; so, Rachel put the phone in my hand. To my surprise, I was greeted in Hebrew. It was the Israel Ambassador! He asked how I was doing. I told him I was a bit scared, but in some ways, the shooting reminded me of home. He laughed. I asked how he, his family, and the embassy staff were managing. I knew that they lived close to the epicenter of the "coup." He said that everyone was "safe". However, he knew that I was in a less secure area. He wanted to know exactly how to get to us if evacuation was necessary. I had no idea how to describe where we were located. He asked to speak with Rachel. There were no words adequate to describe my emotions at that moment. I felt happy, grateful, relieved, and touched by the fact that the Israel Ambassador took it upon himself to inquire about my welfare. Everyone in the apartment was amazed that the Israel Ambassador, himself, took such personal concern for the wellbeing of Israel's citizens. To me, this was a way of bringing honor and recognition to the Creator. G-d has commanded us how to treat each other, in every aspect of our lives. He has also given us specific instructions to save any Jew in captivity.

During the continuation of my conversation with the ambassador, I made arrangements with him to meet with someone in order to exchange the C.I. francs I had for dollars. I was afraid that they would be worthless in light of the situation. The person who wanted to exchange the money needed C.I. francs to pay his hotel bill.

The hotel was on the extreme opposite side of town, as far away from Riveria Place as possible and still be within the city limits. It was decided that Rachel and Dora would accompany me, and Mani would stay home with Nesya. (It might not be safe for him to venture out.) Anyway, Rachel was familiar with the area; so, it was decided that she would take me there, and on the way back, we would go to Soco Cey to stock up on necessities. Rachel was still traumatized by the previous "coup" when her family and house guests were trapped in the ULE without even the basic food items and other necessities.

The silence outside was deafening. Only army trucks were on the streets, their canvas walls tied to the tops of their metal frames. The soldiers, sitting on rows of wooden benches, had their rifles loaded and ready for action. Quietly, I said The Travelers Prayer, before we got into the only taxi available. As we proceeded down the road, we came upon many roadblocks and detours. The soldiers manning these posts looked very menacing. They looked as if they had been hardened by many years of war, and all sense of human decency had been incised from their hearts. Shooting at any object they fancied would probably be just an amusing sport. Burnt-out vehicles were strewn along the way. The huge military police compound on the route to Riveria Place was totally gutted by fire. The longer we traveled, the more uneasy I felt. I did not want to be so far away from Nesya and "home."

Finally arriving at the hotel, gave me an awful feeling of total dis-orientation. The contrast between the carnage we had seen along the road and the idyllic setting of the hotel almost completely overwhelmed me, to the point that I felt that I was on the verge of a major nervous breakdown. The hotel was luxurious by all standards. The oval boulevard at its entrance was beautifully landscaped with magnificent colorful tropical flowers. The sun was glistening upon the swimming pool, which looked like a huge coin peacefully resting upon the lush green grass which surrounded it.

The interior of the hotel was just as impressive as the exterior. However, it exuded an uncomfortable, eery feeling because there were no guests in the lobby. It was totally deserted except for a few workers, busying themselves with imaginary work. I somehow felt like Alice in Wonderland, trying to figure out where I was, where I was supposed to go, and at the same time, I had to be careful not to make a wrong turn and end up in some scary hole where mischief was waiting to accost me. The instructions I had received from the ambassador were to call a certain number and say, "Tell Yosi I am here." The person who answered the phone said that Yosi would be down soon. "Soon" turned out to be more than 45 minutes.

Everytime the elevator doors opened, I looked with anticipation. Most of the time, only hotel workers exited them; and when someone else came out of the elevator, they did not seem to be looking for anyone. Finally, almost out of nowhere, three well-tanned tall Israelis appeared in the lobby. They walked over to where we were sitting and sat down. No introductions were made. They asked a few simple questions about how long I had been in Abidjan and when I was planning to return home, to Israel. "As soon as possible" was all I could answer. The "small talk" ended when one of the three stood up and said that the transaction would take place upstairs. Once we stood up, no other words were spoken. We got into the elevator, and one of the men pushed the button for the fourth floor. Once on the fourth floor, we walked the length of the hexagon-shaped corridor. Finally, the three stopped in front of one of the rooms. One of them knocked. From inside, I heard a muffled "כן" ("ken" – i.e. "yes"). The fellow who knocked mumbled something softly, and then the door opened. The young man standing behind the door motioned for us to enter. One of the three offered us glasses of water, which we gladly accepted. As I drank the water, I looked around at the seven or eight men, sitting or standing in different parts of the rather small room. Their presence stirred in me a feeling of safety, a feeling which had been missing in the last few hours, and it was strongly needed and welcomed for me to function effectively. While enjoying those few minutes of comfort and calmness, I was asked a few mundane questions, like where I lived in Israel and for how long. They also asked me about my daughter and when I was planning to return to Israel. I promptly replied, "As soon as possible!" Everyone laughed. Then, Yosi said, "Well, I don't want to detain you. I understand you have about $500 in CIS francs. Here is $300. Keep the rest of your money in CIS francs. You might need them." I removed the colorful CIS francs from my money belt and handed him the equivalent of $300. "Toda" (i.e. "thanks"), we both replied. At that point, we were escorted to the door. I had hoped that one of them would accompany us to the lobby. I wanted to extend, for as long as possible, the feeling of security I had had in this period of extreme madness, but as the door closed behind us, I felt us sinking down into the ugly reality which surrounded us. I took a deep breath, and with a sense of determination, I walked towards the elevator and pushed the button. Once inside, Dora pushed the button "down." The elevator door closed; the elevator jerked a bit and began to descend, seeming to symbolize what lay ahead of us. When the elevator door opened at the lobby, we were almost blinded by the bright sunlight. Where had the sun been when we had entered the hotel an hour ago? We stepped out of the elevator and onto the plush carpet which muffled our footsteps. It was almost as if we did not exist. We were just souls invisible to the world around us. We could come and go, and no one would be aware that we had trod there.

The sun outside the hotel lobby was even stronger. It took us a few seconds to adjust to its brilliancy. We looked at our environs, which refused to acknowledge the turmoil of the civil/military upheaval going on around us. It was determined to remain tranquil. We walked across the hotel's vacant parking lot and out to the main street to try to find a taxi.

Finding a taxi had never been a problem before the "coup," but now the only moving traffic was military vehicles. We crisscrossed the main intersections, trying to find the most strategic point to stand to get a taxi. We began to feel despair. How long would we be stranded there? Rachel suggested that we walk a few blocks and try to find a pay phone to order a taxi. Army jeeps were posted at most of the main intersections. The soldiers who were standing on all corners looked ready to shoot anyone who approached them. Dora was assertive enough to approach one of them and ask where there was a pay phone. The soldier hardly acknowledged her presence or her question. He just pointed down the street on his right-hand side. We walked in the direction that he had indicated, and soon we found an enclosure with several pay phones. Each of us ran to a phone to see if it was working. Finally, Rachel found one that was. However, any attempt to dial a number was met with a busy signal. While Rachel kept trying to dial numbers in hope that someone would answer and try to send us a taxi, I just stood like a little lost child, staring down at the glistening pavement, not knowing what to do with myself.

Finally, as if out of nowhere, a yellow taxi appeared. I don't remember ever seeing a yellow taxi. This kind of reminded me of a Kafka setting- a New York City Yellow Cab in the center of an African city, during a military upheaval. How odd! All of us ran towards it immediately. Dora told the driver to take us to Soco Cey. We wanted to stock up on supplies while we still had the chance.

When we arrived at Soco Cey, the huge parking lot was almost completely empty. I wondered if this was because people had come earlier and emptied the shelves of needed supplies, or maybe, the army or the rebels had looted the stores. Once inside, there was a lack of hustle and bustle, for which Soco Cey was noted. The few people inside the mall did not seem to notice each other. When we entered the supermarket, we saw several people scurrying about, quickly making their choices and heading towards the check-out counters. The strange thing was that most of the people in the supermarket were military personnel, loading their carts, mostly with huge chunks of frozen meat. I thought, "What do they know that we don't know?" It looked like they were preparing for an extended period of upheaval.

Dora, Rachel, and I each took a cart and headed towards a different section of the supermarket. Rachel looked for household staples and cleaning supplies, while Dora took the last of the yogurts and bottled water. I checked the can-goods section and frozen food section. It didn't take us long to fill our carts, mainly because supplies were limited and few people were there to impede our progress. I prayed that when we left the mall, there would not be trouble getting a taxi. To our surprise, there were several taxis waiting outside. It almost seemed like a normal day.

"Normal" was not exactly the right word to describe the next part of our day. The taxi driver had to take many detour routes. Some of the roads were blocked by the military and other roads were so badly damaged that cars could not navigate on them. I was surprised to see a road sign indicating that we were near Treichville. Treichville was **not** in the direction of Riveria Place. This area seemed to be one of the areas most heavily hit, though, now, few military vehicles could be seen "protecting" the region. The taxi driver tried not to drive into the main section of Treichville but rather to stick to the outskirts of the town. Even so, there was enough evidence that the rebels and counter-rebels had had a field day there. The open-air market, the daytime home of the poorest of the poor was almost a ghost town –with one major difference. The ghosts were still there and very visible. Both the rebels and counter-rebels never tried to hide what they did. They slaughtered civilians to instill fear into anyone who might oppose them. Men would be stripped down to their undergarments, forced to kneel on the ground with their hands tied behind their backs. Their heads would be immersed in wooden buckets filled with acid. On the street corners where drug dealers and pimps once stood, headless corps would be tied to lampposts, their body-fluids oozing from every orifice, thus, adding to the stench that usually hung over Treichville. On the knolls just outside Treichville, bamboo cages were placed. What once had been a human life was now merely a skeleton with hungry rats roaming over it, emitting strange noises as they smelled the blood before devouring the last bits of flesh. It seems that when people are so often exposed to atrocities, they cease to feel any emotion that would connect them to the suffering of another human being. This must be a way to survive – self-preservation. In some ways, I, too, felt a type of alienation, a detachment because the scope of suffering was so great, it could have overwhelmed me, and I would not have been able to function. I had to maintain my inner-strength in order to deal with the situation I was in, survive it, and return to Israel – with my daughter. I had to keep my mind focused on my goal in order to succeed.

After leaving Treichville, the driver found a more direct route to Riveria Place. This route was a familiar one, the one which passed by the police compound, near the furniture workshops. In the past, when we had passed by the compound, it had always been a hub of activities. I must say, I was not surprised to see that it had been gutted by fire. Were the people who operated it rebels or counter-rebels? I was totally confused as to the division between the two groups. How were they parceling out their country and for what purpose? Would there be anyone left to benefit from their warrior efforts?

As I was thinking these thoughts, the taxi pulled into the parking lot of Riveria Place. Dora ran up to the apartment to request assistance to carry the bags and bags of items we had bought. The last time I counted them, there were 14 huge shopping bags, overflowing with essential goods. When everything had been carried up to the apartment, Dora, Rachel, and I could not do anymore. The other residents put everything away.

Mani handed me Nesya, who seemed to have missed me a lot. She put her arms around my neck and would not let me go. I found a place on the floor, near the sofa, and I cuddled with her. There was not really much else to do.

Everyone was waiting for some kind of news report to be broadcasted. Finally, there was a strange noise coming from the television. It was an eery sound like that of a horror movie. The T.V. screen was still blank. After several minutes of this annoying sound, a "test-signal" appeared on the screen. Bold letters flashed across the screen, saying "The Head of the Government will soon make a statement." Then, the staged presentation began, while in the background, the eery sound continued. The Head of the Government was dressed in full military garb. He spoke gravely about the attempt to overthrow his government. This had occurred only six months after he had overthrown the officially elected government. He made himself sound like an abused, misunderstood head-of-state, who only wanted the best for his country and his people. He contracted a look on his face which was supposed to convey how hurt he was by the attempt to overthrow his government.

Then, he "shared" with the public scenes from the battle sites, so that we could see the ghastly carnage of war around us. A burnt shell of a tank was teetering precariously on the berm of the road which descended to the lagoon. Coagulated scorched blood looked like open veins spewing their contents down the side of the tank. It came together in congealed pools underneath the tank's caterpillar tracks. To further incite the public to anger, to hate those who were against him, he showed the "culprits." Several young men, handcuffed and stripped down to their underpants, stood in front of the camera. Some stared blankly at the camera; some looked dazed, and some looked terrified. Another scene was of counter-rebels being herded together, beaten, and their sides punctured by bayoneted rifles. They were then forced to climb onto open-back army trucks. Some were teetering on the verge of collapse or death. The news broadcast, commencing with the speech of the Head-of-State, was shown over and over again for the entire evening. Each time it would start with a news bulletin, flashing in bright colors, declaring "Here is the latest update of the news." Finally, everyone got tired of this psychological teasing and retired to their rooms. Though all of us were exhausted, none of us could sleep. Hearing shooting in the distance did not contribute to our efforts to escape from this emotional turmoil. I was certain that everyone was lying in bed, staring at the ceiling, anxious about what might happen next. Somehow, boredom took over, and I, at least, managed to doze off.

Early the next morning, the phone rang, making all of us jump to our feet. The call was for me. My kibbutz father had heard about the "coup" and he was very worried about us. I don't know what happened to me, but all I could do was laugh hysterically. I could tell by the tone of his voice he was confused by my behavior. I am not sure if I laughed because of stress or because of the incredulous situation I was in. For some of my family and friends this was a "typical" event for me. Jokingly, people used to say of me that I never could do anything "normal." Something that should have been a fairly straightforward activity would invariably turn into some helter-skelter unforeseen saga. So, here I was *again*, trying to do something "ordinary," and it turned into a civil war! After having laughed for several minutes, I was able to calm down enough to tell him what was happening and that we were safe – in the meantime. I asked him about the news broadcast in Israel to see if the outside world was better informed than we were. I don't even remember what he said. All I really wanted to know was if he knew how I was going to get out of there. He said he was working on it and for me not to do anything which was unnecessary. I did not understand what he meant by that, but I promised I would try to be careful. We ended the conversation with the salutation, "Soon back in Israel!"

Since everyone in ULE was fully awake, as could be predicted, we went to sit in front of the television. As if programmed robots, we all took our usual places on the sofa, the few chairs, and the floor. Just like the night before, the news broadcast repeated itself again and again, but then, someone noticed that it was possible to read the lips of those handcuffed, scantily clad prisoners. There was a voice-over to what they were saying. What they were actually saying was that they had been held in prison for several weeks prior to the "coup." The night before the "coup" they were herded onto open-bed trucks and taken to the official living quarters of the Head-of-State. There, they were beaten and **_re-arrested!_** We all looked at each other in astonishment. This whole "coup" was fabricated in order to strengthen the Head-of-State's position and popularity! This was incredulous. I was deeply shocked that a person could care so much about himself that he would wontedly cause the death of hundreds, even thousands, of people he purported to care about. How could he destroy his nation's towns, villages, natural resources, and economic stability and advancement in order to increase his popularity among the people and fortify his personal standing among them? A megalomaniac this malicious and egotistical would certainly stop at nothing to maintain his position. This thought sent chills up and down my spine. I wondered how many other people watching the broadcast had picked-up on what was actually happening. For some reason, this new reality disturbed me more than the "coup" itself. I wondered how many citizens were secretly expressing how much they hated him and his smooth-talking, patronizing manner. They probably hate the "counter-rebels" just as much, looking upon them as the scum of the earth, only interested in Power (with a capital P) and money. As the word would filter down that the "coup" was rigged, the Head-of-State would be more hated, and another group of authentic counter-rebels would eventually bring about a true "coup," causing more damage to the country and its resources and more loss of life. One thing for sure, I did not intend to be around to witness any more turmoil.

In all this uproar, I forgot about the deadline for getting the documents from Liberia and presenting them to the Israel Embassy. "Rachel!" I shouted, "what about the documents from Liberia?!" She stopped in the middle of taking a pot off the stove. "Oh!" she exclaimed. "What are we going to do?!" At that point, everyone turned his attention from the fake news broadcast to our more pressing issue. Rachel would have to make a long distance call to her friends at the Red Cross to see if they had been successful in getting the necessary papers. Then, the papers would have to be faxed to Abidjan. After receiving them, we would have to get them to the Israel Embassy within the next 24 hours. With all the pressure, we almost forgot what was happening around us outside. Then, one of the residents noticed military vehicles moving slowly down the street in front of the apartments buildings. No one knew which side they were on - rebels or counter-rebels. The soldiers sitting in the back of the trucks were armed with bayoneted rifles in prone position. We all looked at each other. If the fax had been sent, would we be able to go out and retrieve it at the shop that was a short distance away? Would it be safe to leave the neighborhood? Too many un-answered questions!! I felt some panic churning around in my stomach. I silently commanded myself to calm down. First things first! I asked Rachel if she could call the Red Cross in Liberia and find out if they were able to reach Nesya's biological mother. Rachel handed over to one of the residents the pot she was still holding. Before she picked up the phone, she paused for a moment. I was certain she was worried that phone reception was still being intercepted. Would it be safe to place such a call? After a few seconds, the much-hoped-for dial tone could be heard. We all sighed with relief. Rachel's friend sounded both relieved and worried when she heard Rachel's voice. Any questions that Rachel had wanted to ask were deferred because of the endless stream of queries with which she was bombarded by her anxious friend, who was very concerned about our safety. Often, foreign residents are targets of pent-up frustration of both soldiers and civilians. After several minutes of concerned interrogation, Rachel was finally able to ask about our issue. She was told that the documents had been delivered and signed. The Red Cross vehicle was on its way back to the Monrovian office, where they would be promptly faxed to us. This would probably be done in a couple of hours. All we could do was wait.

Waiting can be one of the most excruciating stressful plights that one can endure. A minute seems like an hour, an hour seems like a day, and a day is longer than eternity. Songs are often comforting in these situations. Without conscious intent, I began to hum a Negro Spiritual:

"Blessed quietness, Holy quietness,

What assurance in my soul.

On the stormy sea, G-d speaks to me,

And the billows cease to roll."

These words comforting and helped me put things into perspective and also coaxed me to be cognizant of the fact that the Creator of all things was still in charge, always watching over me, even in such stressful situations.

Those two hours – an eternity- did finally come to an end when the local fax office called us to notify us that a fax had arrived from the Red Cross in Liberia. Upon hearing this spectacular news, all four of us, Mani, Rachel, Dora, and I, almost knocked each other down, trying to get out of the front door. We had to laugh at ourselves. We giggled as we ran down the dark stairwell, groping our way along the broken stucco walls, trying not to fall over each other. Nesya, who was in her baby-carrier on Mani's back seemed to enjoy the bumpy ride, as she clutched Mani's forehead.

There was no one in the fax office when we arrived. Rachel signed to receive the packet, and we all hurried out to the street to flag down a taxi. Rachel grinned and waved to us as we piled in the taxi and instructed the driver to take us downtown. The driver had barely slowed down before we opened the doors, jumped out, and ran towards the entrance of the Israel Embassy. Mani shoved some money through the window to the driver, and began running with Nesya, trying to catch up with us. The guards already knew who we were. They searched us quickly, scanned us, and escorted us to the floor of the ambassador's office. He was standing in the hallway, waiting for us. I thrust the packet into his hands. After removing the papers from the envelope, he scrutinized them and declared, "Perfect!" He then leaned through the reception window, picked up a document and stated, "This is the entrance visa for your daughter. It's good for two weeks only. Do everything you can to take advantage of it. The situation here is precarious." I was so excited and elated; I almost grabbed him and kissed his bald head. I just kept repeating, "Toda! Toda!" (i.e. "Thank you, Thank you!) Baruch HaShem! Baruch HaShem!"

During the entire ride back to Riveria Place, I clutched the paper tightly and stared at it. I was afraid I was dreaming or that it might be caught by a gust of wind and blown out of the taxi window. After arriving at Rachel's everyone danced and sang, while passing Nesya from one person to the other. She found this confusing, and at the same time amusing. For me, the day had ended. Overwrought from the whole ordeal, all I could do was lie in bed and say, "Thank G-d!" I guess everyone realized how much I needed to rest, for they let me sleep until the morning. Exhaustion had allowed me to sleep deeply and peacefully, thus, giving me the strength to cope with the last part of the saga – getting a flight home to Israel.

When I finally woke up the next morning, the first thing I did was jump out of bed to take a look at the visa to be sure it was real and still there. Then, I carried out my morning ritual of washing and praying. I felt that this was especially important in my situation. Each day I had to renew my connection with HaShem (G-d) and strengthen it. I knew that only with G-d's help and guidance had I come this far, and I would need His continuous support to finish my mission – returning home, to Israel, WITH my daughter.

After breakfast, Rachel went to work, and Dora, Mani, and I sat down to solidify our plan of action. Again, we carefully studied our previous embassy/consulate + airline chart. Some things had to be revised.

Chapter Eleven

The Dutch Embassy

The search for embassies and airlines gave me the impression of déjà vu. Hadn't we already been through this? The three embassies, which seemed to have the most promise for getting the necessary permits were the German, Belgian, and Dutch. They all had airlines, which flew from Abidjan. On Wednesday morning we headed out towards the German Embassy. Since the Dutch Embassy was not far away, we had hoped to be able to go to both the German and the Dutch embassies in the same morning. Getting there was not as easy as we would have liked. The taxi driver got "lost" and he circled around the same area several times before he even found the street, and it turned out that he let us out at the wrong end of the street. Already exhausted from the ride, we then had to walk in the hot blazing sun for several blocks. By the time we arrived at the German Embassy, it was a few minutes before their closing time, not that it made much difference, because after a brief look at our documents, we were declined any assistance. This was disheartening, but the fact that it was too late to go to the Dutch Embassy was even more frustrating. It was 12 noon, and the Dutch Embassy's hours were 9:00 -12:00 and 16:00 to 18:00. The embassy was so far from Riveria Place that there was no point in going home and returning later. We were all tired and hungry. We decided to look for a marketplace or supermarket. We, finally, found a supermarket, which seemed to cater to foreign nationals. The first thing we put in our shopping cart was water. The second was diapers. Nesya had managed to wet through all the diapers we had brought. I decided that in order to keep-up my strength, I would buy orange juice. Dora and Mani had a much larger selection of nourishment. After leaving the check-out counter, we found a small public garden to sit in. When I looked around at the area, I felt disoriented. The buildings, which surrounded the garden, seemed more European than African. Even the weather seemed cooler and less tropic. I was not sure what evoked this sense of dislocation more – the buildings or the landscaping of the garden. I tried to pull myself out of this peculiar feeling of hovering in unknown territory, but the feeling was so strong I felt that I was floating outside of my body in "no-man's land." I did not like this sensation. I felt that it was keeping me from functioning, and I would not be able to carry out all the tasks, which lay before me. I stood up and walked around, but that did not relieve this unpleasant feeling. Frankly, I was worried that the stress of my situation had completely worn me down and I was on the brink of having a mental breakdown. I was afraid to speak about my feelings for fear of frightening Dora and Mani. I picked up Nesya, in hope that this would "ground" me. At first, I didn't notice any difference, but gradually I felt like I was "returning to myself." A cool sense of relief seemed to rest on my shoulders and flow down my torso until it reached the soles of my feet. Quietly, I said, "Thank G-d!" I sat down again and looked around at these strange environs. Then, I glanced at my watch. In seven minutes it would be four o'clock! We could start walking towards the Dutch Embassy, which was located nearby, in one of these strangely misplaced buildings. We took the elevator up two floors and found the embassy at the end of the hallway. We entered and waited for the clerk to notice our presence. With a smile, she greeted us and asked how she could help us. I explained our purpose in coming. After examining our papers, she said the magic words I had been waiting to hear for weeks. "You can fly to Amsterdam, to make a transit-stop before continuing on to Israel, and neither you, nor your daughter, need a visa." I stared at her in disbelief. Since I had arrived in Abidjan, everything seemed to have had unexpected twists and turns; there was always some complication, but here, in the Dutch Embassy, everything went quickly and smoothly - for the first time in FIVE WEEKS! All I could say was "WOW!" Then, to be sure that I had not misunderstood, I asked her to repeat what she had said. It took COLLOSAL internal strength to refrain from jumping in the air and dancing around the office. ISRAEL, HERE WE COME!

When we left the office and rode back to Riveria Place, the embassy clerk's words flowed through my head like a beautiful song of liberty. This man-eating African flower, which had held me in its grasp, had finally opened its petals to allow me to fly away. The joy of this thought was incredible. Until now, the future was just some murky abstract notion , to which no reality was attached. Now I knew that I would soon be experiencing my along-waited goal – taking my little daughter home to Israel. When we arrived at the ULE, the looks on our faces spoke more clearly than words. Everyone danced around and sang, shouting out praises to the Almighty. One big hurdle had been overcome. Now, we had to take action to *really* make our victory complete – getting an airline ticket. It was too late to call the KLM ticketing office. This, we would have to leave 'til the next day. I was so fidgety with excitement; I could not sit still. I walked around the flat, carrying Nesya. Then, I took her out to the veranda to watch the sun set. The sunset always splashed streaks of glowing, animated patterns on the lawn below. A cool breeze, from the lagoon, advanced towards us. It made the laundry, hanging from lines, stand up with life. This caught Nesya's attention. She had to touch each piece as she walked along the veranda. Then, she swatted them and giggled as they changed shapes on the line, making shirts and trousers hug each other. I was glad she gave me this distraction, since I was too antsy to do anything constructive.

Evening had finally come. The programs on television mildly entertained everyone. There were several soccer games and several news broadcasts. The local news was primarily about the proposed government elections. Mister Head-of-State found it necessary to declare that there would new elections in a month. He was clever. He wanted the people to believe that he held their interests at heart. He "primed" them for the elections by frequently broadcasting the national anthem, especially before the news was broadcast. The "news" simply showed happy barefoot children, smiling at the camera, while they sat around a big pot of stew, which was generously served to them. The second most frequently featured news report showed dignitaries, wearing flowing traditional gowns, regally taking their places at some convention or political soiree. I found this whole presentation boring and probably offensive to the average citizen. This whole state of affairs irritated me and made me restless. I thought to myself, "At least this is not a permanent situation for me and I won't have to tolerate this non-sense forever. I truly hoped that I would have a chance to rid myself of the negative feelings I had towards "Mother Africa" and regain some semblance of positive perspective. There was not much time left for me to do this, but I at least wanted to try. I wanted to see the beautiful side of this stunning continent. As soon as I would have "ticket-in-hand," I intended to devote some time to exploring at least a tiny portion of this land.

These were my thoughts as I prepared Nesya for bed. In my mind, I ran through the next day's itinerary. I decided to take advantage of the lack of pressure, which always troubled me, and to lie in the bed and just stare at the ceiling. I remembered that as a child, my mother used to play a game with me, in which we identified odd shapes that had formed by reflection of the light or tiny cracks in the paint. When Nesya would be older, I intended to share this game with her. One thing I had noticed in this ceiling was that it had, obviously, been painted several times, and this caused the paint to form blisters, which made the newer layer protrude in uneven patches. From these patches I could imagine all kinds of objects, both animate and inanimate. I entertained myself this way until I fell asleep.

By six o'clock the next morning, I was awakened by the news programs on the radio. There were skirmishes along the northern and western borders of Nigeria. HIV was taking a heavy toll in lives in several of the east Africa and central Africa countries. Nothing was mentioned about the situation in the Ivory Coast. While going through our morning routine, I discussed with Rachel the subject of seeing a little more of the country than downtown Abidjan. I wanted to see a safari, but she did not think this would be possible because the safari tours were all on the other side of the country. She said that there was a zoo right outside Abidjan and she would try to get information about going there. Rachel went off to work, and my comrades and I headed for the KLM ticket office in downtown Abidjan. Booking a flight was just as easy as the experience we had at the Dutch Embassy. Within twenty minutes all arrangements were made. We were scheduled for:

KL2205- arr. AMS 4:10; - dep. AMS 7:20, -arr. TLV 11:00

By noon, we were already back at Riveria Place. Rachel called us to tell us that she had arranged for some relatively short excursions in the area, and if we wanted to, Etienne, a prominent friend of Rachel's, would come and take us to some interesting sites in the area. He could pick us up at four o'clock. I was thrilled at the idea. Dora quickly fed Nesya and put her to bed. Mani took a shower and plopped himself in front of the television, and I scrutinized all of our official documents to be sure nothing had been overlooked. I ate some rice I had prepared in the morning and some canned sardines which had the OU kosher symbol. These sardines I had found in Soco Cey on our last trip there.

Etienne was quite prompt. When I saw him, I was impressed by his demeanor. He was a perfect blend of French elegance and African genteel character. His smile was one of gracious sincere warmth. After having tea and sitting with us for what was considered the appropriate amount of time, he suggested that we start our journey before it would be too late to enjoy the view. Etienne was a proud Ivorian. He knew his country well. He shared with us some of the many characteristic features of the Ivory Coast. One thing that struct me as anomalous was the way the country had been developed. When we left Abidjan, we immediately entered a very modern motorway. There was a feeling of traveling in time to the same place several decades later. The international road signs also had instructions in French. The terrain was magnificent. There was no hint of poverty. After about half an hour, Etienne pulled off of the freeway, and immediately we found ourselves in an area where the roads were scarcely paved. Mani asked if we could stop at a roadside stand and buy some fresh fruit. This stand looked as if it had been created just for us. It was colorful and picturesque, and there was no one else around. I had a weird feeling that as soon as we drove away, it would disappear from the landscape. From here on, the road was just a gravel path. We bumped and lurched along for what seemed an endless amount of time, and the next thing I knew, we were again on a beautiful, modern expressway. I looked out the rear window to see if where we had been really existed. I expected it to fold up like one of those children "pop-up" books. Etienne had had in mind to show us the richness and multiplicity with which his country was blessed. We had not known that our last adventure of the day would be the most extraordinary.

Again, Etienne pulled off the freeway, but the connecting road was moderately comfortable. This road twisted and turned, inclined and declined through the lush green landscape. Finally, a small stucco white structure could be seen in the distance. Etienne informed us that that was where we were headed. None of us asked any questions. We were enjoying the outing. As we approached the building, we were stupefied to see a huge red sign announcing "Snake Museum." Mani, Dora, and I looked at each other. I think we were all anxious, but at the same time, curious. Etienne parked the car, got out, and opened the car doors for us. When it was time for me to get out, I felt my knees buckling under me. The museum proprietor came over to us and asked how many tickets we wished to purchase. I guess he thought that Dora and I would not want to enter the museum. Etienne turned and looked at us. With composure on the outside, and panic screaming on the inside, we both said we would be accompanying them inside. Inside the cement building the air was cool and moist, and quiet shouted out at us. There were four separate rooms, each one more frightening than the previous one. The first had pictures on the walls, showing the different types of snakes in the area. Then, there was a picture classifying the snakes according to their venom: poisonous and non-poisonous. The second room contained new-born and baby snakes. The third room contained larger non-poisonous snakes. They slithered around their cages, basically, ignoring us. The last room contained the poisonous snakes. There were vipers, pythons, and cobras of all sizes. When we entered the room, some of them became agitated. They "snaked" along the cage floors and wriggled up the cage doors (which did not look sturdy), as if trying to find a way to escape. Some of them seemed to bang themselves against the mesh-screen cage door, as if to challenge us. When the proprietor enticed the cobra, and the cobra raised the upper part of his body and lunged forward, I was ready to leave. I had had enough adventure for the day. Before I vented my thoughts, everyone else said that they felt it was time to go. The proprietor had a hint of a smile on his chiseled face. He thanked us for coming and invited us to come again. I said that I might do that if I was in the area. I thought to myself, "That will never happen."

When we left the snake museum, I was completely exhausted. I even fell asleep on the way back to Riveria Place. I woke up as we pulled into the parking lot. Etienne informed us that he would like to take us to the local zoo the next day. Zoo animals could also be dangerous, but they did not arouse in me the same fear I felt in the snake museum. I told Etienne that we/I would be looking forward to seeing a real African zoo. In my mind, I pictured it as a "contained" safari. That night was much like the night before. It seemed like I had no worries and I could relax a bit. I crawled into bed beside Nesya and immediately fell asleep.

The next morning, I woke up with a feeling of anticipation. We were going to the zoo – a real African zoo. I wanted to see how Nesya would respond to seeing lions, tigers and bears. On the way there, I sat back and enjoyed the scenery. I wanted to retain in my memory as much of Africa as I could. I wanted to be able to look back and have some pleasant memories of Africa.

THE ZOO

Sometimes people should not have high expectations. This would prevent great disappointment. I guess I had expected an African zoo to be a bit like The Bronx Zoo. After we walked through the gate, I was wondering when we would get to the "good" part. This zoo looked as if it had been frozen in time (and the animals did too.) It was in need of serious repair. The entrance gate was rickety, and the paths were crumbling. The paint on the walls was peeling, and the cages stood on platforms, which were disintegrating from age. There were hardly any zoo keepers attending the area. The animals inside the zoo looked as old as the structure itself. The lion hardly had the strength to roll over in his cage. I felt so sorry for the bear; I wanted to help him walk from one side of his cage to the other. Then, the thought popped into my mind that this was more like a senior-citizens' home for animals. I tried to get Nesya excited about seeing the animals, but I think she sensed my emotions because she hardly paid attention to the animals. She preferred to spend her time jumping over the cracks in the pavement. Luckily, the zoo was not very large, and it did not take a lot of time to roam around the whole area. This was good, since the only "roaming" that was done in this zoo was done by the people who visited it. I was immensely relieved to get back to the ULE. I really appreciated Etienne's effort to be hospitable. However, this day, only re-enforced my ambivalent feelings about "Mother Africa."

That evening, I spent my time packing and re-packing our luggage. I did not want to forget anything. I wanted to be sure that I had packed all of Nesya's things in a way which would be easy to access them. Then, the thought struck me; once I get to the airport in Abidjan, I will be on my own – a new mother coping by herself. I would have no one to turn to to ask for advice. I would have to use my "motherly instincts" (whatever that meant) to deal with all situations which may arise. Fear and panic began to knag at my self-confidence. I knew I had to find a way to cope. One of the strengths of Judaism is the Book of Psalms. Psalms 91 is considered the Psalm of Protection. I needed protection *from* myself - as well as from the world around me.

THE 91ST PSALMS

"Whoever sits in the refuge of the Most High, he shall dwell in the [protective] shade of the Almighty. I will say of HaShem "[He is] my refuge and my fortress, my G-d, I will trust Him." For He will deliver you from the ensnaring trap, from devastating pestilence. With His pinion He will cover you, and beneath His wings you will be protected; His truth is shield and armor. You shall not fear the terror of night; nor of the arrow that flies by day; nor the pestilence that walks in gloom; nor the destroyer who lays waste at noon. A thousand may fall victim at your side and a myriad at your right hand, but to you it shall not approach. You will merely peer with your eyes and you will see the retribution of the wicked. Because [you said], "You HaShem, are my refuge," you have made the Most High your abode. No evil will befall you, nor will any plague come near your tent. He will charge His angels for your, to protect you in all you ways. On [their] palms they will carry you, lest you strike your foot against a stone. Upon the lion and the viper you will tread; you will trample the young lion and the serpent. For he has yearned for Me and I will deliver him; I will elevate him because he knows My Name. He will call upon Me and I will answer him, I am with him in distress; I will release him and I will bring him honor. With long life will I satisfy him, and I will show him My salvation."

My self-confidence began to rise. I was about 90% sure I could manage, but what about that 10% of uncertainty? Well, I found that assurance in a Negro Spiritual, "His Eye is on the Sparrow."

HIS EYE IS ON THE SPARROW

Why should I feel discouraged
Why should the shadows come
Why should my heart be lonely
And long for my earthly home?
When G-d is my portion
My constant friend is He
His eye is on the sparrow
And I know He watches me
His eye is on the sparrow
And I know He watches me

Chorus:

I sing because I'm happy
I sing because I'm free
For His eye is on the sparrow
And I know He watches me

"Let not your heart be troubled,"
His tender words I hear,
And resting on His goodness
I loose my doubts and fears.
Tho' by the path He leadeth
But one step I may see
His eye is on the sparrow
And I know He watches me
His eye is on the sparrow
And I know He watches me.

Chorus:

I sing because I'm happy
I sing because I'm free
For His eye is on the sparrow
And I know He watches me

Whenever I am tempted
Whenever clouds arise
When song gives place to sighing
When hope within me dies
I draw the closer to Him
For care He sets me free
His eye is on the sparrow
And I know He watches me
His eye is on the sparrow
And I know He watches me

Chapter Twelve

Out of Africa and WITH MY DAUGHTER

When we are at the brink of a paramount event in our lives, we often lack inner peace. Stress builds up inside and permeates all of our senses. Again, I found myself at loose ends the Shabbat before my scheduled departure. Here I was hours away from the moment I had been waiting for, for more than six weeks. I had to try to regain Shabbat serenity. I knew that I needed to pray. This required great effort because of all the hustle and bustle in the ULE. I searched for a place where I could have relative quiet. In a corner of our shared bedroom, I tried to recite the morning blessings from my tiny prayer book. There was not enough light; so, I began to pray the prayers as I remembered them. The first blessing was: "Blessed are You, our G-d, King of the universe, Who has given the rooster the ability to distinguish between day and night." I pondered this blessing. Knowing that there is G-d in charge, keeping everything functioning, was a comfort to me. The days were passing, and they were propelling me closer to home, closer to taking my daughter to the land of our forefathers – Israel! The second blessing is: "Blessed are You, our   G-d, King of the universe, Who opens the eyes of the blind." When having to recite the prayers from memory, additional mental effort is required to stay focused. I felt certain that during my stay in Abidjan, my vision had been clouded by the uncertainty of the situation. Now, I had a chance to pause, look around, and see how the hand of G-d was involved in every aspect of my predicament. My eyes were open to the awesomeness of His greatness. The third blessing is: "Blessed are You, our G-d, King of the universe, Who frees the captive." I had been in captivity, not knowing how I would return to Israel with my daughter. Now, a different reality was beginning to set in. I was being released - and with the satisfaction that I had accomplished my goal. Captivity is a two-faced vice: physical captivity and mental captivity. There are times when we are in physical captivity, over which we have no control. It is misleading because it gives us the impression that all is lost and that we are at the total mercy of others. Mental captivity is inflicted on us by ourselves. However, this form of captivity we do have control over. When we activate our mental freedom, we can come up with ways of gaining physical freedom. How? Our thoughts propel us beyond our physical bondage. When we know that something or someone is out there busy working to obtain our physical freedom, we have already overcome our physical bondage. It is all a matter of time. Focus is of utmost importance. Mentally, we break through the bars behind which we are confined. When we are far enough away, we look back and laugh at those who tried to enslave us and we smile with satisfaction that we are the victors and not they. My "captors" had not been the army or the rebels, but rather a force of human evil, which was opposing the force of human dignity and universal good. Most wars are fought because of not honouring human dignity. After being enmeshed in this human drama of capricious folly, I had to struggle to maintain lucidity of mind, knowing that no situation is eternal. I had to have the strength and courage to find solutions to overcome all obstacles. I had to keep my eyes open always, for a means of escape. So, here I/we were at the ebb of our escape to freedom. I had to be mentally prepared and physically prepared for any hardships or unexpected road blocks. This could be taken at its literal meaning. The fourth blessing is: "Blessed are You, our G-d, who lefts up those bowed down and makes them stand straight." This is how I envisioned myself entering the airport, passing through "Security", and boarding the plane. I would walk with dignity and assurance that G-d would be with me all the way. The next blessing is: " Blessed are You, our G-d, Who clothes the naked." Yes, I had been naked, exposed to the winds of war and the elements of change. However, G-d had girded me with protection from all forces and elements. Blessing number six is: "Blessed are You, our G-d, King of the universe, Who gives strength to the tired." I was not only tired; I was exhausted, both mentally and physically, but now, I was feeling a new surge of strength and energy, by realizing that I had come this far by faith. In the back of my mind was an old Negro Spiritual, "We've Come This Far by Faith." The next stanza is "Oh, don't turn around. We've come this far by faith." This is exactly where I stood right then. There was not turning around. I was going to make it across the finish line. The seventh blessing is: "Blessed are You, our G-d, King of the universe, Who makes the land surface above the waters." I thought of the lagoon, which could be seen in the distance. It was there in all its beauty, but part of its beauty was the land which encompassed it. The land gave man firm footing, which allowed him to move forward. The eighth blessing is: "Blessed are You, our G-d, Who prepares man's steps." So often we are unaware of this. Each of our steps is being guided by G-d. We just have to be in tune with our surroundings. Sometimes, when walking in the sand, we see foot prints ahead of us. In really unstable areas, we often walk in the foot prints of the one who preceded us. This is how G-d is for us. When the ground is unstable, He walks ahead of us to lead the way and prepare secure footing for us. The ninth blessing is: "Blessed are You, our G-d, King of the universe, Who provides for all my needs." This was definitely true in my situation. These initial blessings helped me gain insight to a higher order of being. They prepared me for my last moments in Abidjan and for the final leg of my journey home, to Israel. After finishing my prayers, I had regained the Shabbat serenity that I needed so much. I set a corner of the communal dining room table, so that it somehow resembled my Shabbat table at home. Then, I took out the little bottle of grape juice that I had so lovingly packed in my suitcase. I sat Nesya in the high chair, and as I was about to make Kiddush, the rest of the residents of the house came and stood reverently around the table. I was glad for this communal atmosphere on what was to be my *last* Shabbat in Abidjan. I tried to preserve the internal peace I had and sustain it throughout the rest of the day. At the same time, I wanted to preserve a visual memory of the ULE; so, I walked around the apartment to capture and engrave in my mind the sights, the sounds, and the smells. I stared out the window at the lagoon. This sight was imprinted in my brain like a golden blue icon. It had somehow shared some of my most intimate thoughts and feelings.

Shabbat was almost over. I had had to "guesstimate" the time Shabbat ended because I didn't have a calendar which lists the hours of the beginning and ending of Shabbat. Our sparse belongings were already packed and ready to go. A tingling sense of excitement coursed through my body. I could hardly contain myself. I was only able to make a quick quiet blessing for ending the Shabbat. Everyone, except

Dora, crowded around us to say "good-bye" and wish us G-d's speed in the final part of our journey. Mani and Dora were planning to accompany us to the airport, but Dora was nowhere to be found. The residents began to do a room by room search. Finally, one of the female residents informed me that Dora would be coming out of her room in a couple of minutes. We waited as long as we could, and then Mani collected our luggage, and I put Nesya in her stroller-backpack, and we made our way down the dark narrow staircase – for the last time. Outside, the taxi was waiting for us. Before I got in, I looked back to see if Dora was coming, but there was no sight of her. My heart ached at not being able to say "good-bye" and thank her for all her help and kindness. As I seated myself in the back seat of the taxi, I looked again to see if I could get a glimpse of Dora. She was not there. I sighed and said a silent "good-bye" in the direction of the Riveria Place flat that had been my home for more than six weeks. I wondered if I would see any of these wonderful people again. I said a quiet prayer that they would be safe.

The ride to the airport seemed like a silent movie I was participating in. For some reason, the airport seemed darker and more sinister than when I arrived and when I had made my previous futile attempt to leave the country. The air was very heavy. The heat pressed down on us as if to crush us into the hot asphalt. The humidity was stifling. I stood outside the taxi for a moment, in order to catch my breath. Mani busied himself with paying the taxi driver and removing our luggage from the trunk of the car. Nesya had fallen asleep, as she usually did when we travelled in a car. Mani walked with us towards the airport terminal. All of a sudden, a huge burly soldier stood in front of him and told him he could go no farther. He asked Mani if he was planning to board a flight, and when Mani said "no", the soldier said that that was as far as he could go. From here, I was on my own. There was still about 100 meters before I reached the barrier outside the terminal. I could not understand why soldiers were not allowing people to approach the barrier outside the terminal. I looked back at Mani, and he waved at me. I needed his feeling of assurance. I hoped he would wait outside for a while to see if I got through security okay.

Inside the airport, an atmosphere of terror and alarm reigned. Only a few small low-watt lights lit the ceiling, and they hardly provided enough light to maneuver through the reception area. I had no idea where I was supposed to go. Then, a "police officer" motioned for me to come to him. We communicated mostly with sign language. I understood that he wanted to see our passports and our tickets. He had a very angry look on his face, but I was not sure towards whom his anger was directed. He looked at our passports and tickets and then grabbed them out of my hands. This startled me. He walked away and didn't look back. Then, I saw he was showing our papers to another officer. This officer also scrutinized them thoroughly, and then handed them back to the first officer. He walked back over to me, handed our documents back to me and pointed me towards a flimsy wooden partition. I struggled to drag our luggage and balance Nesya whose head was flopping from side to side as I walked. Behind the partition was a row of benches. I understood that I was supposed to wait there, but for what, I did not know. I looked around for someone to turn to to explain to me what I was supposed to do. I saw no one who looked like he was "official;" so, I just sat down and waited. Finally, from the far side of the barrier, I heard footsteps. They sounded as if the person was wearing army boots. I waited to see who was approaching. Several soldiers, very aware of their authority and power walked into the area where I was sitting. They looked around, scrutinizing the area, as if they were looking for someone in particular. Then, they looked at me. Three of the soldiers came towards me. In heavy accented English, one asked to see our passports and flight tickets. I handed him my papers. He turned his back towards me and showed the documents to the others. They, in turn, looked at them. Then, one of the soldiers handed the papers back to me. One of the other soldiers pointed to a partition on the other side of the room. Behind this partition several people were seating with their luggage nearby at their feet. No one was talking. Everyone was staring straight ahead. I looked around for a place to sit, and I found a primitive wooden bench to the left side of those sitting in the "waiting-room." I still didn't know what to expect next. A few minutes later, a young Asian fellow came and sat down beside me. He struck up a conversation. His face was beaming as he described his experience in the Ivory Coast. He told me that he was from Korea and that he had come to the Ivory Coast, hoping to have a spiritual experience. He had not been disappointed. He seemed to be on a spiritual high as he spoke of the spiritual enlightenment he had gained while in Africa. All I could think of was what a contrast his feelings towards Africa were to those of mine. I had come here with a feeling of "going home to mother Africa that would nourish me." Now, all I could think about was getting out of Africa as quickly as possible. I listened to him with curiosity and wonder. What kind of emotional/spiritual attachment could an Asian find in Africa. He wanted me to tell him what my spiritual experience was in Africa. I was hesitant to share with him anything that I had experienced. First of all, I had not yet totally sorted out my feelings. Secondly, I did not know how much time we would be sitting together. Nor, was I sure that there were no eavesdropping devices in the area. All I shared with him was that it was quite emotional to be in Africa and that this was expected of any African-American visiting Africa for the first time.

About 30-40 minutes later, an announcement was made over the loud-speaker that we could now leave the terminal and walk towards the airplane which was waiting to the right of the exit. I started to run. I almost forgot about my Korean comrade. He began running after me and took some of my luggage from me so that I could run faster. We literally ran the 200 meters to the plane. I don't know if we caused a panic, but I saw others also running towards the plane. He helped me place my luggage in the belly of the plane, and stayed with me until we were allowed to board. The last time I saw my new Korean buddy was when he was helping me up the steps into the plane. Then, he disappeared.

Once inside the plane, the flight attendant looked at my boarding pass and directed me to our seats. I placed Nesya in the seat beside the window. She seemed like she was ready for a new adventure. I put earphones on her and chose a music station which I thought she would like. As other people boarded the plane, they stopped and looked at her in amusement. She was leaning towards the window, her head against the seat, legs crossed, and tapping her little feet to the rhythm of the music. The flight attendant came by again to stand and look at her. After I settled myself down beside her, I concentrated on the "take-off." I felt like I was trying to *will* the pilot to rev up the engine and begin the take-off. I waited impatiently. The flight attendant came around again and handed me a little gift for Nesya. It included a bib and a few toys and also a pacifier. Nesya had never had a pacifier, and I was interested to see what she would do with one. I gave it to her and she just held it in her hand. I put it between her lips, but she would not suck on it. I gently pushed it into her mouth, and she spit it out onto the floor. I looked into the gift bag to see if there was something else I could entertain her with. Actually, I was trying to entertain myself. Finally, the pilot announced that we should prepare for lift-off. Emotionally, I had been prepared for this moment since yesterday. I put my head against the back of the seat, put Nesya's hand in mine, closed my eyes, and waited for the roar of the engine, signalling the beginning of taxiing down the runway. There was a certain feeling of "unreality." Sometimes we wait for something for so long that when it finally becomes a reality, we are dumbstruck. Soon after our ascent, Nesya fell asleep. As I was dozing off to sleep, a Negro Spiritual gently began to flow into my semi-consciousness: "Oh freedom, oh freedom, oh freedom over me." With its soothing melody and comforting words, I drifted into a deep, relaxing sleep, a sleep of "no-worries." I had been released from captivity, and now I was on my way home.

A few hours later when the pilot's announcement to prepare for landing pierced my sleep, I was not sure where I was. My eye lids were so heavy; I had to force them open. My body felt like a block of lead attached to the seat. Nesya, who was curled up beside me, was still in a deep sleep. I wiped the sweat from her forehead, and she stirred a bit. I raised the window shade to get a glimpse of Amsterdam before we landed. Then, I decided to quickly change Nesya's diaper so that I wouldn't be covered with pee-pee during the time it took to leave the plane and enter the waiting room lobby. The flight attendant helped me gather my things and prepare for landing. The sensation one gets during take-off and landing is exhilarating. There is a feeling of accomplishment and satisfaction. This was especially true for me that day. As we landed I stared out the window to get a glimpse of the city. I knew that I would only see the airport once we were on ground. A few minutes after landing and the shuttle port was attached to the plane, the flight attendants opened the door. A gust of "new" air entered the plane. This also sent a sense of excitement coursing through my body. In just a few hours, I/we would be boarding another flight for Israel. I sighed with relief at the thought. "Almost there."

The four hours in the airport seemed like an eternity. The clocks never seemed to advance to another time. I wandered around the huge airport trying to find something interesting to do and maybe something kosher to eat. I remembered that in Israel there were cookies from Holland, which had "kosher" printed on the lids of the round metal containers. I could not find any here. I went into some of the shops which sold food. The odor of pungent cheeses and cured ham made me nauseous. I forced myself to go into one of them to look for fruit that we might be able to eat. Aah, bananas! They seemed to almost jump at me. I bought several bananas and left the shop to look for a place where we could sit and eat. I found a place near a young woman who had a son of mixed lineage. No one stared at them, except two middle- aged men from a WASP background. I overheard them discussing where they thought she was from. Then, one of the men said to the other, "How could she let that happen to her?!" I wondered if they also thought something derogatory about Nesya and me. After enjoying the treat of "forbidden" fruit, we strolled around the terminal trying to find something interesting to do. My feet were swollen, and every step was an effort, but I had to do something to stave off the boredom. Finally, it was time to board the plane. Tears welled up inside me when I saw the Israeli flag on the side of the plane. Yes! Yes! This was the final stage of our journey! We were on our way HOME!

Once inside the plane, a sense of accomplishment and pride tweaked my soul. Six and a half weeks ago, I had set out on an undertaking, which I knew was going to change my life. The treasure of my mission was cuddled up next to me. I had "given birth" in an atypical way. Nevertheless, I had become a mother, and "I did it my way." I leaned my head back on the seat and listened to the conversations around me. People were speaking many different languages, but among them all, Hebrew flowed like mystical music to my ears – and to my heart. I enjoyed every moment of the flight. Soon, we were going to land. I felt like I would burst with joy. Jews had waited for centuries to return to their homeland. I only had to wait six and a half weeks, and that seemed like an unbearable eternity. But, here I was, returning to the land of my dreams, having fulfilled my dream of becoming a mother. G d is great!

This time when the pilot announced that it was time to prepare for landing, I was ready. As the plane began to descend over the Tel-Aviv sky-line, I held Nesya as close to me as possible. I told her we were almost home. I told her to look out the window so that she could see Israel as the angels see it. We would be landing on holy ground in just a few minutes. I knew that once I collected our luggage, Abba Yoske and Ima Yafa (whom Nesya would have the privilege to call "Saba " and "Savta") would be waiting for us at the exit. I could no longer hold back the tears. I wept from the bottom of my soul. I wept from every cell in my body. I wept for all the Jews who never had the fortune to return to their homeland. I wept for Nesya, who was chosen from among many to live her life in the Land of Israel. G-D IS GREAT AND HIS MERCY ENDURES FOREVER!

Printed in the USA
CPSIA information can be obtained
at www.ICGtesting.com
LVHW021622120424
777218LV00002B/265